ADD MORE

TO YOUR LIFE

ADD MORE

TO YOUR LIFE

A HIP
GUIDE TO
HAPPINESS

GABRIELLE
BERNSTEIN

Published in the United States of America by
QNY, an imprint of the Hammond World Atlas Corporation,
part of the Langenscheidt Publishing Group,
Long Island City, New York
www.langenscheidt.com

QNY and the QNY colophon are trademarks of the American Map Corporation

Book Design by Linda Kosarin
Photos: Sam Bassett

Catalog-in-Publication Data is available from the Library of Congress
ISBN 978-0843-716559

Printed and bound in the United States of America

First edition
1 3 5 7 9 10 8 6 4 2

To Lauren Zussman,
I will continue to carry your message.
Thank you for shining your light
on this world.

ACKNOWLEDGMENTS

First and foremost, I thank my family. Mom, you are my soul mate and my best friend. Thank you for teaching me the true meaning of love and inner guidance. Dad, you are my teacher and my biggest fan. Thank you for your faith in my vision and your dedication to the light. My brother, Max, there is no one cooler than you, bro. Aunt Hattie, thank you for your endless edits, coaching and inspiration. Grammy, thank you for reminding me that light can shine even through a simple paint stroke. My stepbrother, Scott, and my sister-in-law, Emily, I feel blessed to have you in my life. To my stepfather, Michael, thank you for your endless encouragement and support. To my stepmother, Joyce, our spiritual connection will last forever. Grampy, Poppy and Grandma, thank you for guiding me from above.

To Joe Watson, you are my mentor and one of my dearest friends. I'm a lucky girl to have a guide like you! To Karen Salmansohn, thank you for crowning me the ~ing Girl and paving my path in the publishing world. To my mentors, Ray Sansouci, David Ronick, Billy Diggins, Kris Carr and Rha Goddess, thank you for helping me manifest my dreams.

To my power posse of miracle workers, you all know who you are! Each of your names are inside the frame on page 9, powerfully holding space for love. You have inspired every lesson, every story and every word in this book. You are my teachers and my sisters.

To my dear friend Micaela Ezra, the light in you ignites the light in me.

To my ~ing buddy Zach Rocklin, you have taught me more than you can imagine. Most importantly, you have taught me the true meaning of "holy love."

To those who have helped create this book. I thank Michele Martin, Nel Yomtov, Gina Garza, Jennifer Fragleasso and the entire Langenscheidt Publishing Group family. Thank you for believing in the importance of this message and being my partners on this mission. To my manager, the Lion, Peter Miller and Adrienne Rosado, thank you for your endless roars. With immense gratitude, I thank my dear friend Sam Basset for your incredible photographs. I thank my soul sister, Haleh Roubeni, for styling me with love. To Bevin Reilly, thank you for the hours you spent in my kitchen reviewing every word and exercise in this book. I thank every ~ing Expert who contributed to this book. With endless amounts of love and gratitude, I thank Bonnie Bauman, my editor, word coach, teacher, ~ing buddy and friend. Thank you for holding my hand through this process. Keep on bouncing.

To PS 50, 7:30 AM, you are my family. I thank Bill and all his friends for being my bridge back to life. I thank Elaine Abromovitch, Dr. Rick Barnett and Deborah Miller for helping me grow into the woman I am today.

I thank Heather Cumming and Medium Joao for opening my heart, spirit and soul to the light. My life is forever changed thanks to you. I thank my guides, Sol, Lisa, Merlin, Joan, Anne and J—thank you for holding my hand as I walk over the bridge; I know you have my back. I have endless gratitude and thanks for those who have inspired me most: Marianne Williamson, Dr.

Wayne Dyer, Shakti Gawain and Louise Hay. I hope to carry your messages in true ~ing girl style. Thank you for lighting my path.

Finally, I thank Helen Schucman and William Thetford for the willingness and dedication to give birth to *A Course in Miracles*. Thank you for being a channel for the light.

For daily ~ing tips and correspondence, feel free to visit me at www.addmoreing.com.

Kelly Adams	Nitika Chopra
Jill Reiling	Peg Samuel
Allison Rapson	Sera Beak
Angela Armstrong	Lindsey Eckstein
Kristin McClement	Johanna Benotti
Bevin Reilly	Sara Clemence
Joanna Loewi	Natalie Berthold
Ariele Fierman	Kelsea Brennan
Erin Frankel	Latham Thomas
Kerin Nadler	Nadirah Charles
Justyna Laboza	Meredith Levick
Erica Ellis	Leesa Hubbel
Lauren Badouris	Chelsi Kosarin
Miceala Ezra	Nora Walsh
Francesca Padilla	Dana Watson
Kajal Desai	Leanne Wong
Gina Lorenzo	Saira Caridad
Emily French	Emily Cassaro
Jenny Sansouci	The Miracle Workers Power Posse
Kirsten Hill	
Kassie Johnson	Brooke Emory

CONTENTS

PREFACE

Hello, my new friend. I'm super-psyched that you dug the cover of my book enough to pick it up! Right now I bet you're thinking, "Who the heck is that angel-winged girl on a skateboard in the middle of a busy New York City street, and what's that big grin on her face all about?" Well, in case it isn't obvious, *she* is *me;* Gabrielle Bernstein, and the reason for the grin is that I am happy. I am complete, I am whole and I live for my life! I choose to perceive the world with love. My life feels like a *happy dream* that I'm psyched to wake up for daily.

I was not always this enthusiastic about life. In fact, five years ago I was trapped in darkness and felt my only recourse was to scream my way out. At the time, I was twenty-five and running my own public relations firm in Manhattan. I was your stereotypical middle-class, young New Yorker. On the outside I had all the trappings necessary for happiness: a great family, a great job, great friends. But on the inside, I wasn't happy. Back then, all my focus was on validating the outside world's perceptions of me: What do you do for a living? Who are you dating? What clubs can you get into? These were the things that mattered.

I was full of insecurities, booze and Subway sandwiches. My perception of happiness was a pill, a boyfriend or a new notch on the belt of life's necessary "accomplishments." My mantra was: "The harder I push and the louder I scream, the further I will get." I was obsessed with the *when I have*s. When I have a new boyfriend . . . When I have more money . . . When I sign that client . . . *then* I will be happy. When my *when I have*s became *I have*s, I still felt unsatisfied, and I turned to drugs and alcohol to fill the void. I spent an entire year chasing fleeting highs only to end up with a nasty drug addiction.

I remember the exact date that I hit rock bottom. It was October 2, 2005. I woke up hungover, strung out and ashamed of what I'd done the night before. I heard the clashing sounds of a garbage truck in the street outside my apartment and a steady stream of voices from people headed to work or to the gym. I was headed nowhere. It was then, over my pounding headache, I heard my intuition say, "Stop searching for happiness on the outside. Clean up, and you will find it on the inside." That day I chose a life of sobriety and decided to seek my source of happiness from within.

It was then that I put the brakes on my fast-paced New York lifestyle and developed a new, healthy addiction. I became a metaphysics junkie! And just as the Buddhist proverb promises that "When the student is ready, the master appears," my master, or masters, appeared in the form of a group of happiness gurus—Marianne Williamson, Dr. Wayne Dyer, Louise Hay and Shakti Gawain. I followed their guidance, took their suggestions and shifted my perceptions. Things got way better, *fast*.

It wasn't long before another teacher came into my life, bestselling author and radio personality, Karen Salmansohn. I met Karen at one of her lectures and immediately felt a connection. I knew she had a SIRIUS Satellite Radio show called "Be Happy, Dammit." I wanted to learn from her. So the proactive entrepreneur in me spoke up and offered to be of service. Much to my delight, she took me up on my offer. Within weeks Karen had taken me under her angel wings and begun to guide me as a full-fledged mentor. She introduced me to rad people and even invited me to be a guest on her show. She had a new segment in the works called "Add More ~ing to Your Life," and she thought it might be a good fit for me. Her concept was: *the more experiences you have, the happier you will be.* Stay active—dancing, sailing, skiing, experiencing—and life gets more fun. For the first segment of her new show, I reported on a recent surfing adventure I'd had in Hawaii. Karen and I riffed for thirty minutes on the happiness, Zen moments and life tools I acquired from surf*ing*. The show was a hit! Before long, Karen christened me the official "~*ing* girl," and asked that I report each week on unique ~*ing* activities.

As the ~*ing* girl, I got mov*ing*. I moved fast and I moved slow. I spent time on the water, on the ground and in the air. In some cases, I relied on my upper body strength, in others I needed to focus on balance, or surfacing my inner sexiness. When I first began my ~*ing* explorations, one of my favorite go-to activities was jumping on the trampoline. I would spend hours jumping until I reached a cathartic moment of release. Before long, the happiness of my ~*ing*-filled life led me to find joy in many old activities from my childhood. I started unicycling, rollerblading and surfing again. While each ~*ing*-directed activity required a different mind-set and focus, at the end of the day, what they all had in common was that they took me out of my head and into a state of bliss.

I discovered that when I was in that state, I became completely detached from my surroundings. I found myself in a place that can only be described as "flow." My flow moments felt like time was suspended and I was completely engaged in each activity. I felt at those times that, as Bob Marley would say, "Everything's gonna be alright." Committed to exploring the depths of my ~ing, I began to follow each adventure with a meditation. The meditation was a time to reflect on what I'd learned or released in my ~ing adventure. During those moments, I was able to let go of old feelings of insecurity, fear and sadness.

What I soon came to realize was that my ~ing experiences were guiding me to change lifelong patterns. ~Ing was actually allowing me to get out of my own way! Each ~ing activity had become a beautiful opportunity for healing an antiquated issue in my life. Take unicycling, for example. I first learned how to ride a unicycle when I was in a circus arts program in middle school. Riding a unicycle is just like riding a bike in that years can go by without riding, and you can just hop right back on and regain that muscle memory. When my ~ing explorations compelled me to buy a unicycle seventeen years after I had last ridden one, I literally rode it out of the store. But regardless of my middle school training and the memories of my muscles, this ~ing activity still required my full attention. To keep from falling off the wobbling unicycle, I had to focus completely on balance. In my head, I recited: *"I am calm and balanced."* The more I repeated those words, the more I believed them, and the more I felt them to be true.

As I continued my daily practice of unicycling while focusing my attention on the thought of calm and balance, I started to notice that I was beginning to feel more balanced in other areas of my life as well. When work became overwhelmingly hectic and I couldn't find time for myself, I envisioned myself on my unicycle and mentally repeated my unicycling mantra: *"I am calm and balanced."* This mantra mixed with the physical activity guided me away from many unnecessary meltdowns. By adding more ~ing to my life, I had discovered a way to set myself free of obsessive negative thoughts!

What I was basically doing was practicing new thought patterns, the same way you practice any skill. My positive mantras were like mental push-ups. And because I had a physical activity to attach my mantras to, I was able to grasp the feeling both physically and mentally. I could turn to this as needed and access the feeling in my body and the words in my heart. One reinforced the other. Over time, I began to see positive changes in my life as a result, and the best part was that I had managed to have a ton of fun while making those changes!

As a result of engaging in physical activity, positive affirmations, creative visualization and meditation, I began to feel moments of inspiration. I was inspired to write, develop new business ideas and learn new physical activities. That's when I came to realize that ~ing was so much more than just finding happiness through experiences—it was a method for clearing my mind and opening to receive inner guidance. Inner guidance was my ~ing! And I was diggin' it. This turned into a daily ~ing practice of mental and physical reconditioning.

With this daily practice, my life is now much different than it was on that October day back in 2005. My personal commitment to ~ing was what led me to where I am today. I was guided back to joy through my dedication to physical activity, positive affirmations, creative visualization and meditation. ~Ing became the wind behind my new angel wings and continues to guide me. Today I am a motivational speaker, life coach and author. I am a glass-half-full kind of girl. I am a unicyclist, a mentor, an entrepreneur, a lover of life and a voice for my generation. I turned my will over to the ~ing process and rewrote the script of my life.

My mission in this lifetime is to help guide my generation to shift their search for happiness from the outside to the inside. I want to help you get out of your own way. How will I do this? As a channel for the universe, I download and translate important information. As a mouthpiece, I share a hip and powerful message. Let's go, Generations X and Y, it's time to add more ~*ing*!

Expect miracles,
Gabrielle, aka "The ~*ing* girl"

~*ing*TRODUCTION

Now that you've made the decision to explore the process of adding more ~*ing* to your life, you're probably wondering what the plan is. Well, you've come to the right place! The purpose of this book is to help you shine light on the darker areas of life and create positive change. My work life, coaching hundreds of people (individually and in groups), has armed me with the necessary chops to stand behind my methods. I'll guide you through the process I have worked hard to perfect during my many months of ~*ing* girl train*ing*—a process I have dubbed, the "~*ing* Equation." Here's a sneak peek:

Rethink*ing* + Mov*ing* + Receiv*ing* x 30 days = Chang*ing*

The ~*ing* Equation is a thirty-day adventurous repetition of physical activity, deliberate positive affirmations and creative visualization. The ~*ing* Equation will bulldoze negative thought patterns and create positive change so you can move forward and live an awesome life. The beauty of the ~*ing* Equation is that it can be applied to an infinite number of areas in life to effect positive change. The twelve chapters in this book cover specific issues that affect our generation; issues such as feeling stuck, being involved in difficult relationships, harboring fear of failure or success, and addiction. Here is a more grounded explanation (pun intended): Say you hate your job but don't have the confidence to look for another, or maybe you're in a relationship and it's not working for you, but you're too afraid of being alone to risk rocking the boat to fix things. You can apply the ~*ing* Equation to either of these challenges, and the outcome will be the clearing away of all of the negative obstacles in your mind that are blocking you from finding your dream job or fixing your relationship issues.

The steps in the ~*ing* Equation can be used interchangeably. The Equation is laid out throughout the book in the exact order below, though from time to time it may be adjusted for the sake of a specific chapter's lesson. The thirty-day repetition is required for full-blown transformation. Indeed, neurobiological studies show that thirty days of repeating new behavior reprograms your brain by reversing neural pathways. It's this reversal that changes your patterns and behaviors, and therefore your life. The goal of applying the ~*ing* Equation to different aspects of your life is to clear your channel of all the static, so that you can receive inner guidance.

STEP-BY-STEP ~*ing*STRUCTIONS TO THE ~*ing* EQUATION

STEP ONE: Rethink*ing*

The process of rethink*ing* is all about retelling your story. The unhealed areas of your life are the ego's playground for nasty thoughts (the ego is the nasty voice of fear). In order to change your negative thought patterns, you will actively replace your negative thoughts with loving ideas. These loving ideas are called "affirmations." The process of rethink*ing* allows you to turn every negative thought into a positive one, using myriad tools to help you change your mind. Each conscious decision to change your mind takes you one step closer to reconditioning your brain and changing your life. This step alone will help you achieve big changes in your life.

STEP TWO: Rethink*ing* + Mov*ing*

In step two of the ~*ing* Equation, you add mov*ing*. By layering your affirmations with physical activities, you will shift the way your body responds to your mind. The ego's negative stories from the past live deeper than your thoughts; they inhabit your mind and body. Therefore, I've matched up specific physical activities with the different areas of life covered in each chapter to allow you to change those negative thought patterns on both a mind and body level. For example, if you need to let go of an old fearful belief, you will use danc*ing* to move it through you. Or if your life is off-balance, I suggest jumping on a trampoline. However, there are many activities that apply to different issues, and the ~*ing* Equation is not limited to my suggestions. If you have a certain interest in a specific activity that you dig, then by all means ~*ing* with it! The key is to find activities that guide you to release and empower you to change.

The Equation calls for you to combine rethinking and moving for at least twenty minutes. Doing this will lead you to the ~*ing* *zone*. This is when the energy of your mind and body flow together. It's a wonderfully endorphin-charged kinda feeling, very much like the one you might experience after a great run. In the ~*ing* *zone*, your mind is free and your body is released, leaving you able to access your intuition. This is a time to hear your *inner guidance* and listen to your truthful voice.

STEP THREE: Receiving (Meditating + ~*ing write*)

While you are in the ~*ing zone,* I will guide you into the final step of the Equation: receiv*ing.* This step is a combination of mediat*ing* and stream of conscious writing (~*ing writing*). Each of these activities are opportunities for you to maximize the clarity you receive in the ~*ing zone.* When your mind is clear you can receive truthful thoughts, come up with inspiring ideas and honor your intuition.

You'll begin receiv*ing* by meditat*ing.* If when you think of meditation, you think of a potbellied Buddha on a pillow, drop that idea and welcome a new vision. In the ~*ing* girl's world there is nothing cooler than meditat*ing.* So let go of any preconceived notions you may have of meditation, hang tight, follow my lead and be willing to experience something new. And don't worry if you're a meditation virgin! I've made it supereasy for you. All you have to do is download my guided meditations off of addmoreing.com and allow me to guide you. (If you don't have an iPod you can simply turn on some of your favorite mellow music (preferably without lyrics) in the background.) We're going on a journey through your subconscious brain, and the point of the meditat*ing* step is to allow you to let go of your left brain's practicality and welcome your right brain's intuition and creativity.

What's the point of making this switch? The intuitive right brain is the side with the voice that, when allowed to speak up, says stuff like, "You don't like your job, so it's time to start following your passion," or "You're ready to let go of that old pattern of X, Y or Z." Meditation is a great way to allow your right brain to speak up and be heard. Thanks to the physical and mental work of steps one, two and three, thoughts that were in the way have been silenced, allowing you to hear your *inner guide.* The meditation in step three is crucial because it is an opportunity for you to slow down enough to receive this guidance from within.

Immediately following your meditation I will guide you directly into a stream-of- conscious writing exercise which I've termed "~ing writing." Each ~ing write is an opportunity for you to spill your unconscious thoughts onto the page. To help you put pen to paper and get started, I will provide you with a topic. Your job is simple: Just reflect on the topic by writing freely. Let your pen flow across the page and allow your mind to release its thoughts. The ~ing write is super important because it amplifies your receiving. You will be amazed by what comes through your pen and onto the page!

REPEATing

The key element in the Equation is repeating. It is the thirty-day repetition of the ~ing Equation that will allow you to truly experience the results.

Indeed, as a result of my dedication to daily repetition of the ~ing Equation I live an awesome life. The proof that the ~ing Equation works is in the pudding. It has worked to give me a life I never even dreamed was possible, and it will do the same for you, regardless of what your current life challenges may be.

APPLYing

I'm confident that most everyone will find a part of each Equation that will resonate with them. Therefore, I suggest you complete each chapter's version of the ~ing Equation in its entirety. In addition, regardless of where you're at in your life, I strongly suggest you test-drive each Equation in the order that the chapters are laid out. Here's why: Each chapter focuses on adding more ~ing to a particular area of life. The order of the chapters represents what I believe to be the best path, with each chapter focusing on a specific milestone along that path which will help you embrace the next chapter/milestone.

When you apply the ~ing Equation to different areas of your life, fearful thought patterns and limiting beliefs will subside. If you feel stuck or you don't have control of your life, this book will help you get unstuck and learn to release and let life happen. The instances where ~ing can remove your mind's obstacles and change your life for the better are endless. If your obstacle is a lack of confidence, add ~ing and you'll gain confidence; if your obstacle is a grudge against your mother, add ~ing and you'll figure out the forgiveness thing; if your obstacle is a lack of balance in your life, ~ing it and you'll gain the balance you crave. But ~ing isn't just for problem solving; it's also for making sure you're living your life to the fullest. Regardless of where you are in your life right now, there is always room for improvement.

The reason that I can write this book and testify to the ~ing Equation is that I live it. How dare I tell you how to be happy if I'm not truly diggin' my own life? Here's the deal. Today I live a life that I never thought possible. I would say that 95 percent of the time my mind is calm, I'm happy, and I feel comfortable in my skin. I have full confidence in myself and nothing but excitement for my future. In the past, if something didn't work out the way I hoped it would, I would freak. Now if things don't work out the way I projected, I know there is either something better on the horizon or a lesson to learn. The other 5 percent of the time, I'm working through brief encounters with my ego. But thanks to my ~ing practice, I now know how to keep my ego in check. Whenever it tries to tell me a nasty, old story I say, "Thank you for sharing," and then I hit it with some ~ing. I actually have gratitude for these brief encounters with my ego because they keep me dedicated to the ~ing process. I am fully aware that the reason my life is so hooked up today is because I've cleaned up my past perceptions and reprogrammed my brain through ~ing.

Because I can testify to the power of this Equation, I've chosen to share many personal stories throughout the book. In addition, sprinkled throughout are stories from many women I've coached. Each anecdote reflects how the ~ing Equation can positively change the common issues our generation faces. I'm confident that you'll be inspired by many of the stories, and I hope they provide you with powerful examples of the benefits of adding more ~ing to you life.

The desire to cruise through life on a skateboard, while wearing angel wings, didn't happen to me overnight. It took a commitment to happiness—and a lot of work. But don't let that scare you. There is nothing in this life worth attaining that doesn't require effort.

THE PATH TO ADDING MORE ~ing TO YOUR LIFE

Now that I've given you a rundown of the Equation, I'd like to tell you what's in store for you as you turn the pages and begin your journey through this book. Each chapter focuses on a separate issue and provides step-by-step guidance on how to apply the ~ing Equation to effect change within that issue. Each Equation has been slightly altered to best apply to whatever area of life is being addressed. This is the beauty of the Equation; it's meant to be flexible so that it can best tackle whatever area of life it's thrown at. Once you know the ropes you can apply the Equation to any issue at any time. The ~ing Equation in each chapter represents a milestone.

Each of these milestones allows you to better navigate your journey down the path to your ultimate destination, which is adding more ~*ing* to your life. Each chapter builds on the one before it, helping you construct a solid foundation of serenity. In the first half of the book, chapter one to chapter six, I'll help you work through all the hidden feelings and negative habits you've picked up over the years. The second half of the book, chapter seven to chapter twelve, will open your mind to a new understanding of how to get more out of life. You'll learn about the infinite capacity of your own personal energy and the power of your thoughts and feelings. Once you've gotten past these important milestones, I'll teach you how to use this energy for manifestation and co-creating with the Universe. Think of each ~*ing* Equation as a fun adventure that will guide you closer and closer to a rockin' life filled with happiness.

A MIRACULOUS INSPIRATION

Before we get started on the journey of adding more ~*ing* into your life by applying the ~*ing* Equation, I'd first like to explain one of the major inspirations for the ~*ing* process—a book titled *A Course in Miracles*. The *Course* is a self-study metaphysical guide that can be approached in whatever capacity works best for the individual. The *Course* teaches that "An untrained mind can accomplish nothing." The main objective of the *Course* is to guide the student to relinquish the ego (from the *Course*'s perspective, the ego is "quite literally a fearful thought") and commit to aligning all thoughts with love. My experience studying the *Course* has resulted in a full-blown mind cleanse and a super-rockin' life. As soon as I reprogrammed my fearful thought patterns, everything began to change. The most significant change was shifting my perception from fear to love. In addition, I now see all adversity as learning opportunities rather than tragedies. Overall, following the *Course's* suggestions has led me to forgive my past, release my future, and show up for the present with love and faith.

I have revisited the *Course's* text year after year, and as I grow, the language grows with me. In fact, one of my goals in creating the *~ing* Equation was to use the *Course's* philosophies in a modern way. If you dig it, work with it—if you don't, take what you want and leave the rest. This is your journey. Roll with the tools that you vibe with, and feel free to make them your own.

L-*ing*-o

The final tool I want to provide you with to help you in your journey through the book is the following list of important L-*ing*-o that I use throughout. Because these terms might be new to you, the ones I use most often are listed below along with a simple definition of each and an explanation of its *~ing* tie-in.

~Ing: means "inner guidance." *~Ing* is the voice inside of you that screams intuitive loving thoughts and says "bug off" to fear. Throughout the book, you'll notice that "*~ing*" is used interchangeably with "inner guidance." *~Ing* can be used as a noun, as in, "Today I am choosing to add more *~ing* into my life," or as a verb, as in, "*~ing* it, sister!" Here's a bit more about *~ing*: The "new age" hippy in me has been known to correlate *~ing* with inner light, an inner voice, a Higher Self, the source, and, in some cases, God. (I am very aware that the word God might freak you out. But roll with me on this one.) There are many unique ways of referring to your *inner* *guidance*. In her book *The Artists Way*, Julia Cameron beautifully offers the acronym for GOD as, "Good Orderly Direction." My girl Sera Beak aka "Spiritual Cowgirl" and the author of *The Red Book*, refers to ~*ing* as "however you experience the divine— energy, nature, life, love, you, God/dess, Buddha nature, the Wiggling Wow." My dear friend, author and speaker Kris Carr, refers to ~*ing* as "God, Jesus, Buddha, Elvis, etc." Your ~*ing* thoughts sound like this: "Take a nap." "Don't psycho-call him, it's 2 AM." "Stop eating." "Put down the drink and go home. "Get off of Facebook—you love yourself more than that."

Ego: *A Course in Miracles* refers to the ego as "quite literally a fearful thought." These thoughts of fear tell you: "You're not good enough." "Life's difficult." "It's a recession, you can't get a job." "You're too fat." "You're bad in relationships and will be single forever." The ego dwells in the pain of the past, recreates it in the present and projects it onto the future. The ego is the voice of a nasty friend you've been listening to for way too long. Your commitment to ~*ing* will turn down the volume on your ego.

The Law of Attraction: Have you ever found yourself thinking of a friend, and within seconds she or he calls? Or have you ever desired a certain piece of information and that same day were led to a book that explained the info you were seeking? These are day-to-day examples of your attracting power, which are a result of the Law of Attraction. Put simply, like attracts like. If you keep thinking, "I'm going to lose my job," you will lose your job. The same goes for positive thoughts. The ~*ing* process will clean up your attracting power by guiding your thoughts back to the positive.

Universal Energy: The energy of the Universe is inside all of us. Negative thoughts, feelings and beliefs can stop you from receiving its gifts. If you want a rockin' life and are truly willing to accept a new idea, I can teach you how to access this energy inside you. When you ~*ing* enough to receive this energy, you feel a rush of love flood your body and your mind whenever you call it in.

Manifestation: The outward result of an inward intention; the process of turning your desires into form by activating your energy with powerfully focused thoughts and precise vision.

Now that you're down with the L-*ing*-o, we're ready to begin the journey. Strap on some sneakers, pack your notebook, pen and iPod, and get ready for your first ~*ing* adventure!

CHAPTER ONE

Feeling: Surrender
Then Release

The course does not aim at teaching the meaning of love, for that is beyond what can be taught. It does [aim], however, at removing the blocks to the awareness of love's presence, which is your natural inheritance.

—*Introduction*, A Course in Miracles

When Alison was nine years old, she came home from school one afternoon to find that her father had left, taking most of the family's belongings with him. Alison's mother, completely distraught, remained in her room crying for the next two months. Overwhelmed by what was going on, Alison internalized her feelings, and in that way she was able to avoid the reality of what was happening. Despite her efforts to block out the trauma of her parents' divorce, however, the event did have an immediate impact on her: though she had always been superconfident and outgoing, Alison became more reserved and less sure of herself.

Fast forward fifteen years. When Alison came to me for coaching, she gave me the lowdown about her parents' divorce. I was surprised at how nonchalantly she talked about it. Despite the traumatic details she was sharing with me, she seemed virtually unmoved. It was as if she was telling me about a movie she had seen the day before. She then told me what life was currently like for her. She had trouble believing that she was good enough in all areas of her life, particularly in relationships. "Men suck and nothing ever works out," she complained. And she rarely trusted anyone and never allowed people to get close to her. Despite her tough talk, all I could see was an innocent nine-year-old girl begging for relief from a pain buried deep within. I asked her if she had ever dealt with her feelings about her parents' divorce, and she replied, "Oh, yeah, I've been getting over that for years." ("Over it" being the operative words.) From what I deduced from our time together, she had been eating *over it*, thinking *over it* and shopping *over it* for years. Sadly, by burying her feelings about her parents' divorce, Alison had never given herself the opportunity to *heal* from it.

Like Alison, we have all experienced instances where we have buried feelings of hurt and pain instead of dealing with them head-on. The source of your pain may not be as obvious as Alison's. You may not even realize it exists. But I promise you, it's there—although not for long! The purpose of this chapter is to help you uncover your unhealed wounds so that you can face any negative feelings that you have repressed over the years. I understand that this might be new to you. Unfortunately, our culture has not trained us to be comfortable addressing our feelings. We've been trained to think with our left brain's logic and practicality, and ignore our right brain's capacity for delving into our emotions. Therefore, many people go through their lives denying or ignoring their unhealed pain, rather than facing it head-on and thus allowing ourselves to heal.

But first, what's so wrong with burying bad feelings instead of dealing with them head-on? I mean, if those troublesome feelings are locked away somewhere, why's that such a bad thing? Isn't it better than having them racing around in your brain wreaking havoc? The problem with this logic is that repressing feelings is the very thing that *causes* them to wreak havoc! That's because if you don't face your negative or painful feelings, you will remain stuck in the ego's *getting over it* stage, and continue to evade your true healing. Remember the ego? It's that sneaky little bugger that dwells in the pain of the past, re-creates it in the present and projects it onto the future. And the worst part is, you aren't even consciously aware that this is going on! For all you know, the painful feelings are well out of your way, buried down deep where they can't cause you any harm. But all the while, your ego—without your permission or knowledge—has discovered those hidden feelings and collected all of the negative energy from them to use as ammo to make mischief. Most likely, your ego has stirred up a big ole pot of "limiting beliefs" and fed them to you: "I'm unattractive and unlovable." "I'm just not smart enough for that job." "I'm terrible with money and will never get ahead." "I'm just not a person people warm to." "I have issues with food." "I'm lazy." In my profession, I've witnessed many denied feelings turn into limiting beliefs that completely paralyze people from making necessary changes in their lives, or worse, cause them to adopt self-destructive behaviors. But ego is not always that obvious; sometimes it's virtually impossible to know that repressed painful feelings are what's behind a certain negative issue in your life. Oftentimes, the only way to figure this out is to overcome your limiting beliefs, and from there wait to see what the *positive* results will be.

But how can you excavate long-buried bad feelings, especially if you don't even know you have them? The answer: ~*ing!* ~*ing!* ~*ing!* It's time to crank up the ~*ing* Equation, or in the case of this chapter, the Feel*ing* Equation. Here's how it's going to go down: The Feel*ing* Equation is unique in that it has an extra step: feel*ing.* The feel*ing* step will help you identify any old wounds you may be avoiding. Then you will be led to feel. Once you allow yourself to feel, you can then surrender to the healing process. The Feel*ing* Equation will guide you to fearlessly pour some peroxide onto past wounds. The good news is peroxide only stings for a minute, then it makes the wounds start healing! Just think of the quick sting as the crucial step of feel*ing.* Properly cleaning the wound is the hardest. Once you set the healing process in motion, the gaping wound soon becomes a scab, and within weeks it's pink new skin. Within a month, all you have left is a beautiful scar, a gentle reminder of an old lesson.

But before you get started on the Feeling Equation, you'd probably like to know exactly what you can look forward to "changing." And what, if any, inspiration can you expect? Unhealed feelings from the past block you from authentic happiness. On top of that, as new painful feelings crop up, your brain continues its old habit of repressing them. It becomes a vicious cycle: since you've never allowed yourself to actually deal with painful feelings, you haven't developed the skills to do so. You're living your life always burying your negative feelings. As a result, you go through your life talking, thinking and doing over the pain. Meanwhile, swelling deep underneath is a negative voice in your head taunting you with the words "I'm not good enough." Before long, the nagging voice manages to plant this thought, and it takes root as an actual *belief* that you are not good enough.

But there's good news. Applying the Feeling Equation to this area of your life will result in complete thought-changing patterns that will undo any and all of these negative feelings. At the end of the process, in their place will grow feelings of self-love and peace. And the coolest changes might be the ones you never expected. Remember, you're not only ridding yourself of negative feelings— you're also getting rid of the limiting beliefs that were manufactured from the negative energy the bad feelings harbored.

As for the inspiration you can expect: unresolved painful feelings take up a lot of space in your psyche, and once you've cleared out all those painful feelings, you'll have made room for tons of inspiration. My client Molly's first love broke her heart when she found out that for nearly the entire seven years they had been together, he had been unfaithful to her. After they broke up, she did the whole "self-improvement" thing. She got in great shape, got in with some cool new friends and even moved from her college town to New York City, where she got a kick-ass job. But what she hadn't done is deal with the feelings of pain and betrayal her breakup had caused. Tellingly, she had terrible luck with men in the big city.

Then one day, she started getting calls from her ex. Suddenly, all of the feelings of hurt and betrayal that she had buried years before came washing over Molly. For a few days she felt really down. But during that time, she hung out with her best friend, talked out the feelings and had some good cries. Ultimately, she told her ex she was ready to move on and that he should not call again. After this experience, she developed a renewed sense of confidence. It wasn't long after that that she met and fell madly in love with an amazing guy.

Most recently, I've transformed the wounds of my past into beautiful new ways of being. For more than a month, I hung out with the feeling of not being smart enough to write this book. I had an antiquated limiting belief that I wasn't smart, which dated back to the sixth grade when a boy I had a crush on called me stupid. From that point forward I actually believed I was stupid! I tried many tactics for getting over this limiting belief, but the feeling always managed to sneak back in. It blasted me hard when I began the process of writing this book. In order to begin the book, I had to get cozy with the feeling and then release it. Each time the feeling behind the words "I'm not smart enough to be a writer" snuck in, I would melt away the pain by simply feeling it. I'd sit in the feeling and get curious about it. I figured out where the feeling originated, and accepted the untruth behind it. My inner voice, or ~*ing*, told me that I was totally capable of the job ahead; I turned my inner voice up loud enough to drown out the negative limiting belief. By surrendering to the feeling, I was able to heal it.

Now, let's get started down the path of feeling. Before you begin the Feel*ing* Equation, it's important to discover what sort of damage your ego has wrought with your buried negative feelings over the years. Here are a few questions to ask yourself that might help you uncover them: *Do you feel stuck in negative patterns for fear of feeling hurt or disappointed? Do you feel that you are not good enough in some areas of your life? Do you harbor nagging voices in your head that sound like the following: "I don't do well in relationships," "I'm not good enough to succeed in life," "I have difficulty making money"?*

It says in *A Course in Miracles* that "Being afraid seems to be involuntary; something beyond your own control." That is exactly what has happened with your limiting beliefs. These thoughts have become completely beyond your control—they're second nature by now. You identify so closely with them that they embody your perception of yourself. Once you've tapped in to these voices, I want you to accept them for what they are—recycled negative energy from repressed pain, and more importantly, accept them for what they are *not*: THEY ARE NOT THE TRUTH!

THE FEEL*ing* EQUATION:
Thirty Days to Healing

STEP ONE: Feel*ing*

Carl Jung, the founder of analytical psychology, states: "The foundation of all mental illness is the unwillingness to experience legitimate suffering." Therefore, in order to heal it, ya gotta feel it. When you are willing to experience your negative feelings, they release.

Resisting the pain causes more of it. Don't be afraid to feel. It's the fear of the feeling that has kept you from recovering. What I'm asking you to do now is to just rip off the Band-Aid and get curious about the way you feel. Close your eyes and ask yourself the following questions: *How can I describe this feeling? Am I sad, fearful or anxious? Am I all three, and more? Where do I feel this in my body? What does it feel like? Is it raw? Does it have a color? What shape is it? Is it tight? What is underneath it? Is there a word that is associated with it? A person? A time?* Ask yourself anything that will help you identify the feeling underneath your thoughts. Don't push it away, don't think it away—just be with it. By getting curious about your feelings, you may be reconnected with the place in time where they began. For many people, these feelings stem from childhood.

STEP TWO: Rethinking

Now it's time to take those negative feelings and rethink them into positive feelings of self-love. To do this, close your eyes and breathe deeply in through your nose, and out through your mouth. Take a moment to connect to your breath. Then ask yourself: *What are the beliefs I have about myself that are holding me back?* Write down your answers. Cross out the limiting beliefs and write your new affirmations in their place. If your limiting belief is "I am incomplete without a man," reverse it with *"I am complete as I am."* If your limiting belief is "I'm not good enough," reverse it with *"I am wonderful as I am today."* You may want to specify something that you have been trying to release, in which case you can use the affirmation: *"I release _____ and allow my myself to feel my feelings."*

For the next thirty days, hang out with your feelings. When you notice the limiting beliefs come up, just honor how they make you feel for ninety seconds and breathe. A feeling can move through you in ninety seconds. After feeling for a minimum of ninety seconds, call on your reversed affirmation. Say your positive affirmation out loud and continue on with your day. Do this as often as possible.

STEP THREE: Rethinking + Moving

Sometimes our feelings are so deeply buried that we have to physically move them through. Remember, we don't just carry our feelings in our minds and hearts, we lug them around in our bodies too. It's now time to stop dancing *around* your feelings and just dance *with* them. In this step I ask that you apply your new affirmation to some form of dance. You'll find that with dance the real release into clarity comes through in every beat and every rhythmic motion. You can do this dance formation in the comfort of your own home. (Dancing in front of a mirror is one of the joys of life!) You can dance to your own music. Allow your feelings to surface, and with each beat and each movement, release any negative feelings.

I've found dancing to be one of the greatest physical activities for releasing blocked feelings. For instance, I recently experienced incredible emotional release in a dance class at a dance studio called S Factor. This was not your typical dance class. It was founded by dancer and actress Sheila Kelley. Over a decade ago, Sheila was rehearsing for a role as a stripper for the film *Dancing at the Blue Iguana*. Because she wanted to explore the character deeper, she went to a strip club and began taking lessons in pole dancing from the women who worked there. Sheila quickly realized that the movements used in pole dancing are more important than we've been programmed to believe. She came to learn that the moves brought forth an opportunity for internal transformation and emotional healing. "There is a surrender that happens, and you begin to delve into an emotional place," says Sheila.

Since there is no ~*ing* that I won't test-drive, upon reading Sheila's story, I showed up at one of the S Factor locations in New York City. Once the teacher turned off the lights, I felt as if there was no one else in the room. The music began to flood through me. Within minutes, buckets of tears were streaming down my face. My dancing at S Factor took me on a journey to release unhealed feelings from a former relationship. During the class I realized that these feelings dated further back than that one relationship. This realization caused me to dance my way through my timeline of love and the deep-rooted sadness that I'd thought I'd *gotten over*. I was able to release deeply buried feelings.

Another incredible healing dance method is called 5Rhythms, created by Gabrielle Roth. The philosophy behind 5Rhythms is that "when you put the psyche in motion it heals itself." I've witnessed the 5Rhythms dance movement heal many lives. For more on 5Rhythms and S Factor visit www.addmore-ing.com.

STEP FOUR: Receiving (Meditat*ing*/~*ing write*)

Meditat*ing*

Meditation is not just for potbellied Buddhas on a pillow. The results you'll experience from a daily meditation practice are astonishing. I'm here to tell you that five minutes a day spent in stillness with your ~*ing* can transform your life. The concept of stillness might be new to you considering our society's "go out and get it!" mentality. But the fact is, meditation is the most transformational tool in the ~*ing* box. If you are new to this whole meditation thing, don't worry, I've made it simple for you. I've made some tracks of my voice mixed with music to lead you through your meditation. Just plug in and let my voice be your guide. If you don't use an iPod or MP3 player, you can follow the written meditation below, and if you'd like, you can play some ambient music in the background.

MEDITATION SCRIPT:

Take a deep breath, in through your nose and out through your mouth.

Allow your mind to soften, and reconnect with your body.

Identify the area in your body that is holding on to pain.

Take a deep breath into this pain.

Release on the exhale.

As your mind softens, allow your feelings to be your guide.

Gently ask yourself where these feelings came from.

Is there a time period associated with these feelings?

Is there a person or specific situation associated with them?

Let your feelings guide your mind.

As you deepen into the feeling with each breath, identify where your pain came from.

Open your heart and mind to welcome these feelings.

Gently remind yourself that it is completely okay to feel.

Breathe in and feel the feeling.

Breathe out and release.

~ing write

An ~*ing write* is a stream-of-consciousness writing exercise that will release your inner voice. Immediately following the meditation, ~*ing write* in response to your feelings. Write in response to the following questions: *Where are these feelings harbored in my body? Where did they come from? What have they been telling me?* For example, my client Devin's ~*ing write* looked like this: *"My feelings are living in my chest. They are so uncomfortable that it's difficult to breathe. I guess I can describe them as inadequate, ugly and just gross. These feelings are coming from somewhere. I guess from when I was a little girl. I think back to being a little girl and not feeling smart, not feeling pretty, and not feeling as good as my older sister. Not feeling necessary. The majority of the time I felt like no one cared. My overall thought behind these feelings is that I'm just not good enough."*

Take Devin's example and ~*ing write* for fifteen minutes. The discoveries that you uncover in this ~*ing write* will be incorporated into later chapters. Allow yourself to free your mind, release into the feelings and identify their origin. Most importantly, *feel.*

THIRTY DAYS OF FEELi*ng*

Now that I've walked you through the steps of the Feeli*ng* Equation, my hope is that you will adopt it as part of your regular ~*ing* practice. Once you have allowed yourself to acknowledge and feel your true feelings, they will begin to soften. As you continue to allow yourself to feel for the next thirty days, they will begin to release. You won't wipe out these feelings overnight, but one day at a time they will transform. It's kinda like going to the gym: You work out for a week and your muscles are sore. After two weeks you feel a little stronger, and after a month you are in much better shape. It's the repetition of the exercise that brings about the change. Plus, you will free up vast amounts of space to let inspiration in. Thanks to that inspiration, you'll be ready to take on even more ~*ing*!

CHAPTER TWO

Forgiving: Set Yourself Free

Today we practice learning to forgive. If you are willing, you can learn today to take the key to happiness, and use it on your own behalf.

—A Course in Miracles

In my first coaching session with Hanna, she complained of being angry, resentful and stuck in all areas of her life. She believed that life was tough, everyone was out to get her and that her only recourse was to fight back. "All of my problems are the fault of my family and my confining culture. They have made me believe that I have no place in this world other than to be a wife and mother," she said. Hanna's negative reactions to her family only served to fuel the anger and resentment within her. As a result, she remained in an endless cycle of negative feelings toward her family, which negatively affected her work and her relationship with her husband.

I explained to Hanna that one of the best ways to release negativity and resentment was to throw down the "F" word. I raved about the magic "F" word and how I use it when I coach, when I lecture and even when I speak to my mom. I explained that many miraculous moments have stemmed from my use of the word. Peaceful breakups, transformational business deals, powerful shifts in perception—all brought about by my brandishing the mighty "F" word. I asked Hanna to try it out for herself. "Take a deep breath and throw your family a big 'F bomb,'" I instructed. "When you exhale, say '*I forgive you.*'" Hanna laughed, and she responded, "Forgive them! Why should I forgive *them? I'm* the victim here." I explained to Hanna that she would remain the victim if she continued to *choose* to be the victim. And that, unbeknownst to her, her anger toward others hurt her more. I told her that she had been rehearsing the role of victim on a daily basis, and that the cycle couldn't end until she learned to forgive. I made it clear that if her desire was to change her life and be set free from her resentful patterns, forgiveness was in order.

To illustrate for Hanna the importance of forgiveness, I threw down an *~ing* metaphor. I compared her reluctance to forgive to waterskiing—the wrong way. As anyone who has tried it can tell you, the first rule of waterskiing is: If you fall, *immediately* let go of the rope. I first tried waterskiing on Copake Lake, traveling to upstate New York for a day of instruction for my *~ing* girl radio segment. I started off great. I tugged along and willfully managed to stand up on my first try. I loved the feeling of flying over the water with the breeze and the spray hitting my face so much that I never wanted it to end. So once I was up, I was unwilling to let go of the rope. Even when I began to lose control, I gripped the rope tightly and tried to continue skiing. My waterskiing buddies who were watching from the boat were screaming, "Let go of the rope!" But I didn't listen. The boat dragged me along, and even though my arms felt like they were being pulled from their sockets, I refused to let go. The waves were smacking me in the face and crashing over my head. My legs were trembling, and I felt battered and bruised. It would have been easy to blame any number of things for my predicament—the speed of the boat, my equipment, the choppiness of the water. But the truth was, I was my own obstacle that day. After succumbing to the pain in my arms, I finally let go of the rope. And once I released it, I found myself floating freely and peacefully in the water. I lay back and floated in the middle of the warm lake, fully supported by my life preserver. Happiness and relief washed over me.

Holding on to old resentments, habits and situations is just like being dragged along by a powerboat. You might think it's your boyfriend, your mother, your company, your childhood, your friends or your circumstances that are creating whatever state you're stuck in. But you have more power than you realize, or maybe than you're willing to admit.

Hanna dug my metaphor, but I could tell she still wasn't totally buyin' what I was sellin'. She understood that forgiveness would lead to release, but she was still unclear on where to begin. Stuck and a bit confused, she blurted, "This is going to require a miracle!" I replied, "That's exactly what it will take!" In response to this I busted out a quote from *A Course in Miracles*: "Miracles occur naturally as expressions of love." I explained that the miracle of forgiveness stems from an inner shift rather than an outer result. Through the expression of love rather than negativity and fear, the miracle will arise. When you choose to forgive, you release the person and choose a peaceful state of mind over your old chaotic way of thinking. The miracle happens when you change your mind. Though many amazing conditions can result on the outside from the shift, the true miracle occurs on the inside. Thus, each time you forgive someone, you are choosing love over fear and shifting your perception. In Hanna's case, if she wanted to experience more freedom from her family, she had to do her part to set them free in her mind. This concept was tough for her to grasp; therefore, I asked Hanna to let go of the *how* and start to *allow*. Basically, what I meant by this was "chill out and ~*ing* it."

In spite of her initial resistance, Hanna was willing to test-drive the ~*ing* Equation and see what this "experiencing miracles" business was all about. By committing thirty days to the Forgi*ving* Equation, she learned to perceive her family in a much different way. Through her commitment to forgi*ving*, Hanna came to realize that a need to forgive is merely a call for love. When you carry resentment, it is a sure sign that there is love missing from the situation. The forgi*ving* process is designed to teach you that the ego's refusal to forgive is based on illusory perceptions. It feeds off of fear from the past and recreates it in the present. In Hanna's case, she was continuing to replay her fearful memories from childhood into her present. Each time her family invited her to Friday night dinner, she thought she would be sucked back into her old life— even though today that story no longer existed. It only existed in her mind. By forgiving her family for their past behavior, Hanna was able to let go of the old story. She stopped playing the victim. And she began to experience her relationships with the members of her family for what they are today rather than what they were fifteen years ago.

With the slightest willingness, you will receive change. Today you have two choices where forgiveness is concerned: One, continue to be angry and miserable, or two, forgive, let go and be happy. Forgiveness leads to joy and peace of mind. The joy may come right away as an overwhelming feeling of relief or a moment of compassion and genuine love. Or it may take you a while to feel the shift. You might recognize this sense of joy and peace when something happens that would normally bother you greatly, but in that instance, it doesn't faze you at all.

For example, after Hanna committed thirty days to the ~*ing* Equation, she noticed that her family hadn't changed much, but her feelings toward them and how she felt when she was with them had changed. Her family's expectations and backhanded remarks that used to make her crazy no longer affected her emotionally. She was able to release them in the moment and was immediately restored to a state of peace. As a result of Hanna's peaceful reactions, her family slowly began to shift their attitude too. In time, everyone was choosing to love rather than attack. Today, Hanna has full faith in the power of the "F" word. Let Hanna's story be a powerful example: If you're ready to experience the miraculous internal shift of forgiveness, follow my lead in the upcoming thirty-day Forgiv*ing* Equation. Let go of the rope and expect miracles!

Hanna's obsessing, blaming, anger and unforgiving thoughts kept her attached to a speeding boat that was headed straight to unhappiness, by a rope she was unwilling to let go of. Your lack of forgiveness may be as obvious as Hanna's, or it may be more hidden and insidious. You might be thinking, "I'm still angry at my ex-boyfriend, but it doesn't matter because he lives across the country." But if you don't tie up your loose ends of unforgiveness, you will continue to play the victim; maybe not with your ex, but definitely in future relationships. Until you release past hurts through the forgiv*ing* process, you won't be able to create the miraculous change necessary for enjoying life in the present.

If you're ready to make some moves toward that goal, let's begin identif*ying* who you need to forgive. Take a good look around and figure out who needs an "F" bomb thrown their way. To get the ball rolling, whip out your notebook and answer the following questions: *What relationships or memories still cause me to feel acute pain or sadness? What are the negative thoughts my mind turns to repeatedly? Who am I unwilling to forgive?*

There are no right or wrong answers here. The important

thing is to identify the situations so you can begin to let go. If you're having trouble pinpointing the answers to these questions, consider asking close family members or friends for their perspective. Some examples might be:

- "My ex-boyfriend is a cheating liar. I wish he didn't exist."
- "I still feel like my mother doesn't love me enough."
- "I am angry with myself for eating too much and not sticking to my diet."
- "I blame my father for all of my poor choices in men."

THE FORGIVING EQUATION—
Thirty Days to Letting Go

STEP ONE: Rethinking

To begin the forgiving process, I will ask you to see the people you are unable to forgive from a totally different angle. The rethinking process begins with choosing to find compassion for those you need to forgive. Anyone capable of harming someone else is a deeply sad individual. The story below simply outlines the power compassion can have on the way you see other people:

A rabbi and his disciple were walking in the street. A man drove by in a fancy carriage and pushed the rabbi out of his way, into a ditch. The rabbi yelled after the rich merchant: "May you have everything you want!" The disciple asked him, "Rabbi, why did you say that to a man with such horrible behavior?" The rabbi replied, "Because a happy man wouldn't throw a rabbi into a ditch."

The rabbi had the right idea. Believe it or not, it's best to brush yourself off and have compassion for those who have hurt you. Of course, in some cases you may recognize certain people's behavior as totally unforgiveable. For example, forgiving a rapist or a drunk driver who has killed someone you love may be impossible. The best way to look at these situations is not from the perspective of just forgiving their horrifying past behavior, but also forgiving their present and their future. By forgiving these people, you offer them an opportunity to change their lives, and in many cases resurrect their mind to a place where they can be of service to the world.

A powerful example of this is Victoria Ruvolo, a forty-four-year-old office manager, who in the fall of 2004 was driving when a frozen turkey crashed through her windshield, breaking nearly every bone in her face. This assault that could have killed her or severely damaged her brain was the imprudent action of a 19-year-old college student named Ryan. As a result of this harmful, foolish act, Ryan was indicted on first-degree assault and faced up to twenty-five years in prison. Luckily, Victoria's surgeries were successful, and she didn't suffer any permanent damage.

A few months later, Victoria and Ryan met face-to-face for the first time in the courtroom. Ryan was crying as he looked her in the eye and apologized for his actions. In that moment, Victoria called on forgiveness. She embraced him as he sobbed. She reportedly said, "It's okay. It's okay. I just want you to make your life the best it can be." Furthermore, Victoria insisted that the prosecutors agree to give Ryan six months in jail and five years probation rather than a twenty-five-year sentence. Victoria's forgiveness offered Ryan another chance at life. She allowed him to learn a powerful lesson at a young age.

Victoria's actions teach us that forgiveness sets the other person free to right their wrongs in the future. However, the real person she set free was herself. By releasing her anger she learned the true lesson of forgiveness, which is to see everyone with compassion and love regardless of their actions. Most importantly, Victoria taught us that forgiving a horrifying act offers the assailant a miraculous opportunity to change and grow. Learn from Victoria. Strive to have sympathy for people who have caused you harm. If you wish to feel as free as Victoria and the rabbi, it's time to call on some compassion.

Make a Compassion List

Identify the areas where the person or persons on your list are struggling. Be willing to see their side of the story. For instance, "My father didn't receive enough love as a child and therefore doesn't know how to show love properly." Or, "I have compassion for my boss, who is clearly under a lot of pressure and has a hard time expressing her frustration."

See Your Part

Next, it's time to try to see the part you've played in the situation. Figuring out your part might seem too far to reach. You may think you've done nothing wrong and that you are 100 percent the victim. If that's the case, think back to my waterskiing story and how difficult and painful it was for me to hold on to to the rope. I kept holding on to the illusion that if I continued to struggle, the ride would get easier. This false impression is the way of the ego. Your part may be as simple as: "I've been angry for so long, how can I let go of my anger now?" Additionally, it may be very difficult to see your part in the situation because of the other person's actions. Some of you may have been the victim of a sexual assault or physical abuse. I know it is nearly impossible to imagine seeing your part in this. In these cases, your part is simply that you have continued to hold on to the anger. Remember that holding on to the anger is only keeping you stuck in it. See your part in the situation, whether it's a literal action you've taken or merely the unwillingness to let go of the anger. The fearful ego tells us that by holding on to old resentments we protect ourselves from getting hurt again, or "falling." The irony is that the release is in the fall.

Change Your Mind

Now that you've done the heavy lifting, it's time to change your mind. Start by telling a new story and create a forgiveness affirmation. This affirmation can be simply, *I forgive you and I release you.* Or, *I accept that you're suffering too, and I choose to release this.*
Write your forgiveness affirmation: _____.

On a daily basis, for the next thirty days, state your forgiveness affirmation to the universe as soon as you wake up. Recite it again before you go to bed. And for extra points, say it anytime during the day when you find yourself thinking your old thoughts. Next I'm going to ask you to pick up your affirmations and jump rope with them!

STEP TWO: Rethinking + Moving

For thirty days, recite your new thought patterns in conjunction with the daily activity of jumping rope. I chose jumping rope for the forgiving Equation because it ignites a feeling of release. If you try jumping rope for just ten minutes, you will feel a sense of liberation upon letting go of the rope. A simple exercise like this can purge you of your un-forgiving blocks. Remember that you are not limited to my suggested activity—feel free to move with any

~*ing* activity that helps you experience a feeling of release.

Move for at least ten minutes. If you choose to jump rope, after ten minutes you will feel the need to let go of the rope. Let your body get in tune with the feeling of release by simply letting go of the rope.

Fearlessly step outside your comfort zone and enjoy the process. Bring the affirmations you came up with in step one to the activity, or simply recite this affirmation while you move: *I release and I forgive.* Remember that by affirming your new thoughts in conjunction with the ~*ing* activity, you are literally reprogramming the neural pathways in your brain and changing your mind.

STEP THREE: Receiving (Meditating/~*ing write*)

Plug in your iPod and allow my voice to guide you toward forgiveness. (Download the mediation off www.addmoreing.com. Again, if you don't have an iPod or MP3 player, just follow the written meditation below.) The majority of my releasing and forgiving work has been done in the midst of a meditation. Your thoughts and actions play a major role in the forgiveness process, but the power lies in changing your feeling. Your actions and words may shift you to a more loving state, but if the energy behind your actions is unforgiving, the full extent of the miraculous shift won't be realized. When your energy shifts, the people in your life will truly feel it. Meditation is the final step in shifting your energy around forgiveness. Every time I do a forgiveness meditation, it is followed by a miracle. Either the other person calls to apologize, they send a loving text, or I just feel lighter. No matter what the result, it is always wonderful. Regardless of the outer results, the inner results will amaze you.

The following meditation is one that is designed to help you cut the cord of unforgiveness. The cord represents your anger, frustration, pain and fear. This pain no longer serves you, the other person or the overall energy of the universe. Once again, if you are not familiar with meditation, simply relax into it, plug in your iPod and allow my voice to guide you.

In this mediation I will call on some help from my buddy, the Archangel Raphael. (Once again, roll with me on this one. The angels represent beautiful healing properties, and I dig what they stand for.) The Archangel Raphael is a rockin' angel who rules over the heart. He is considered to be the elixir of peace. The peace that lies at the core of your being can be summoned through the act of forgiveness. Raphael brings forth the peace that soothes your anger and calms your mind.

Go to www.addmoreing.com and download the audio meditation, or simply read along.

Take a deep breath in through your nose and out through your mouth.

Hold in your mind whoever you need to forgive. It may even be yourself.

See them before you.

Take a deep breath and say in your mind: *I call on the willingness to forgive you.*

Breathe out—*I choose to release you.*

Take a deep breath—*I forgive you.*

Breathe out—*I release you.*

Take a deep breath—*I forgive you.*

Breathe out—*I release you.*

Envision a black cord between you and the other person.

This cord represents your anger and resentment.

With the willingness to surrender, we call in Archangel Raphael to assist us in cutting this cord.

See in your mind an image of the beautiful angel Raphael.

He flies in with a pair of golden scissors.

He stands over you and gently cuts the cord.

On your exhale, breathe out release as you watch the cord fall to the ground.

With each inhalation, breathe in white light.

This white light will heal you as you release this fearful bondage.

Envision this light pouring through your body, down your head, through your face, down your arms, through your stomach, across your pelvis, through your legs, down extending from your feet, and into the earth.

This white light cleanses your mind and body of all negativity.

It clears your heart so that you can forgive.

Imagine this white light pouring out of your heart.

On the exhalation, extend this light to the person who has caused you pain.

This light is releasing the ego's illusion.

Releasing your fear as it melts away your resentment.

Releasing your attachment.

Breathe in the white light of forgiveness.

And release the white light.

I forgive

I release

I forgive

I release

Continue to repeat this mantra.

~ing write

You have entered the *~ing zone*. The *~ing zone* is the space where your mind is clear, your body has released and you are ready to connect with your intuition. This is a perfect time to download new ideas. The *~ing zone* is the prime state to receive the clear guidance that you might not be able to receive when your mind is jumbled with your efforts to figure things out. This is a state of flow where inspiration beats through your heart and intuition flows through your veins. In this space you can wrap your unforgiving thoughts with love and release your resentments.

Because you are in the *~ing zone* you are ready for the final release. Chose one person, institution or situation that you have been unwilling to forgive, and *~ing write* them a letter. (Remember, an *~ing write* comes out as a stream of consciousness—you don't have to think, just write.) Start at the beginning and write out the entire story of how you were affected by this situation. Allow yourself to write freely. Just let the words flow and get it all out. Be nasty if needed. Grit your teeth. Curse. Say what you need to say.

Conclude the letter by identifying ways that this situation has affected your life positively. For example, it may have guided you to a book or a lecture or some form of self- exploration that has changed your life. The resentment may have been the catalyst for meeting someone who is very special to you now. Think deeply about this and allow yourself to find love in this situation. Pull in some gratitude and wrap the letter with a simple sentence: *"I forgive you and I release you."* Set yourself free and use forgiveness as a pathway toward *inner guidance*, aka your *~ing*.

CHAPTER THREE

Balancing: Bringing Serenity Back

I am leading you to a new kind of experience that you will become less and less willing to deny.

—A Course in Miracles

An astrological reader once told me that I was born in my midlife crisis. This came as no surprise to me. I was twenty at the time, and up to that point, my life had been a series of mini-meltdowns, controlling behavior and addictive extremes. I felt as though I was constantly running from something. It was impossible for me to be at ease if I didn't have a plan. I'd plan every detail of my life, desperately seeking a sense of control. I needed to know the outcome of every situation, and if I didn't have every hour of my day scheduled, I felt like I was crawling out of my skin.

This need for control was evident in all areas of my life—in my relationships, at work, through my eating habits and in my abuse of drugs. Luckily, it ultimately caused me to wind up with an ugly drug addiction. I mean it when I say I was lucky: the drugs and the party scene are what pushed me so far out that my body couldn't run any longer. (One of the countless examples of my physical body helping my mind and spirit figure things out.) In October 2005, I put the brakes on my race to self destruction and surrendered to a path of recovery.

What on earth did I have to recover from? I was raised by great parents, in a nice community, with a solid education. What had I been running from, and how did I end up where I was? In retrospect, I now understand that time in my life very clearly. What I was running from were my feelings. Though my past wounds may sound insignificant to someone who has experienced major trauma, they were deep enough for me to feel the need to run from them. I spent more than a decade avoiding feeling pain from childhood. My pain came from stuff that sounds rather petty: a boy telling me I was stupid, not feeling understood or feeling as though I couldn't share my voice. These situations sound somewhat insignificant, but they were way more than that to me. Like everyone on this planet, at a young age I experienced unpleasant feelings of some kind. The issue wasn't that I'd experienced pain, it was that I *didn't* experience it. I just ran from it. Running from my painful feelings was my way of avoiding ever having to actually experience the pain.

As a result of my ten-year sprint, I got lucky and hit rock bottom. Bottoming out comes in many forms. For one person it might mean ending up in jail; for another, it could just mean waking up one day and deciding that you are done running from your feelings. As a life coach, I've witnessed many folks hit rock bottom. Some people show up at my practice in tears because they have too many negative thoughts and cannot handle them. Others arrive fed up with their eating disorder and ready to make a change. It really doesn't matter what form your bottoming-out takes. All that matters is that you get there. Whenever a client shows up having hit their personal rock bottom, I welcome them and say congratulations! I congratulate them because life only gets super cool when you decide to stop running and start living.

Surprisingly, even at the time, I was psyched to hit rock bottom. I actually felt a sense of relief. And I was thrilled to find out that there was a gentler, more balanced way to live. With an open mind and the willingness to change, I was led to many beautiful books, lectures and teachers who guided me along my path. One afternoon I spent reading *A Course in Miracles*, I remember feeling overwhelmingly inspired by a specific passage. It said, "There is a way of living in the world that is not here, although it seems to be. You do not change appearance, though you smile more frequently. Your forehead is serene; your eyes are quiet." I flipped out over this message. This passage reiterated my deep inner belief that there was a better way to live a serene, more balanced approach to life. The concept of smiling more frequently, with my forehead serene and my eyes softened, embodied my image of true happiness. This vision catapulted my commitment to transform my old behavior. Balance and serenity became my mission, and I was prepared to do whatever it took to get them.

So began my struggle for some semblance of balance in my completely off-kilter life. For me, the balance I sought was aimed at creating a life that was less about drama and a desire to always be in control, and more about having the peace I needed to focus on nurturing the important aspects of my life, such as my own well-being—mental and physical—my meaningful relationships, my career and so on. Although putting down drugs and alcohol made life less dramatic, my ego was still drawn to chaos. Recovery from addictive behavior has been compared to plugging up a flooding boat: when you repair one section of the boat, another section springs a leak.

This was a perfect metaphor for my life. I had put down my addiction to boyfriends and picked up drugs; when I put down the drugs, I picked up food; after I put down food, I picked up work. Because I was still seeking happiness only on the outside, I was endlessly seeking diversions to fill my empty voids. I was still on a mission to avoid my feelings, unbeknownst to myself, and to numb my thoughts by filling them up with plugs from the outside world. And I managed to find a steady supply of plugs.

That's when I realized that finding the balance I craved would require a serious commitment to change. And that my addictive mind was overwhelmed with the nasty voice of my ego. My ego's thoughts had kept me running from my feelings for more than a decade. To demonstrate the power of my ego, my addiction therapist told me that my brain was playing a major role in creating the imbalance in my life. Eager to learn more, I researched this concept further. I learned that my mind had been trained to go in one direction—to the left. The left brain is associated with verbal, logical and analytical thinking. It's super great at placing things into categories, and it thrives off of speech, reading, writing and arithmetic. The linear left brain throws a party when things are placed in sequential order with thoughts like, "I'll get this done first, and cross it off the list so that I can do that second."

Our culture has nurtured our left brain's rational, calculated abilities at the expense of our right brain's intuition and creative capacities. Our modern education has worked hard to strengthen the practical capacities of the left brain. This left-brain mentality has been strongly encouraged through our culture's "achieve, achieve, achieve" mentality.

The right brain, on the other hand, is much more chilled out; it vibes in a nonlinear manner, easily digesting visual, spatial, perceptual and intuitive information. The right-brain processes information in a much hipper way. It sees the big picture and is not as interested in the planning process of "how do I get from here to there." The right brain is totally not interested in patterns or logical planning; it's all about intuition and inner guidance. Cool as a cucumber, the right brain has no problem dealing with ambiguity. Consequently, creative right-brain thinking is difficult to grasp because you're not actually grasping anything—you're just *being*. The right brain has no need to control every outcome, it's happy to be guided.

Once I had a deeper understanding of the two sides of my brain, it was easier to understand how my life had gotten so out of balance. I had been living in a manner that was almost totally directed by my left brain, not giving my right brain any say in how I went about my day-to-day life. Most dangerous of all, I had been completely denying my right brain's intuition. Therefore, my left brain was left to run roughshod over my life, striving to control the outcome of all situations. When it came time to deal with my emotions, its only concern was figuring out how quickly I could get them filed away and move on to the next item on my to-do list. My left brain gave me no time to sit back and process things, get curious about them and ultimately deal with them in a healthy way. So, in effect, my life was out of balance partially as a result of the imbalanced way I was using my brain. In order to get my life in balance, it seemed I needed to figure out how to balance the way I used my mind. This realization, mixed with my willingness to change, got me pumped to make some moves toward that change. And actually, this desire was the first step in tapping into my right brain's power because it was my intuition that was leading me in this undertaking. I was finally allowing my *inner guidance* to take over and put me on the path toward finding a better way to live.

Immediately I went into Sherlock Holmes mode and kicked off a full-fledged investigation. For starters, I asked myself a series of questions. "Where is the balance between practical and creative; calculated and intuitive? How can we learn to function in a way that allows our brain to be in balance? How can I get things done and still be chilled out?" Then, inspired to learn *even more* about balance, I signed up for a workout program at my local gym called "Urban Rebounding." "Rebounding" basically means to bounce back after hitting or colliding with something. "*Urban* Rebounding" calls for jumping on an indoor mini-trampoline; it's a cardiovascular workout that promises less stress on the heart, muscles and joints.

Another of the workout's promises is that rebounding helps to create balance. Being that I was right smack in the middle of an investigation focused on figuring out how to create balance in my life, I had to check it out. I immediately fell in love with the Urban Rebounding workout. And guess what? It *did* help me toward my goal of balancing my life! But you don't just have to take my word for it. Check this out: A Cornell University study looking for a connection between rebounding and balance showed that ten minutes a day spent rebounding increases balance by 68 percent. This research, coupled with my own rebounding experience, was thrilling to me, so I continued to rebound daily in an effort to move closer to my goal of a more balanced life. In order to get the most out of my new rebounding exercise, I memorized the movements taught by the program's founder, J. B. Berns, bought a mini-trampoline for my apartment, put one in my office, and even shipped one up to my mom's house. Whenever I'd have a mini-meltdown, I'd blast music and bounce and rebound my way back to balance.

A result of rebound*ing* (aka jump*ing*) on my trampoline was that I always felt a cathartic release. However, that release was not all that I was after. Remember, my mission for balance included figuring out how to balance the two sides of my brain. So I brought my mind into the mix. I got the feeling my rebounding exercise would also help me with my right–left brain imbalance. Once I had created the *~ing* Equation, I had a way to test out my theory. I began to recite the affirmation, *"I love myself, and I am balanced"* while on the trampoline. This combination succeeded in clearing my mind, and allowing me to feel more balanced in my life. I noticed that situations that used to baffle me became easier to navigate. I became more comfortable not knowing the plan for the weekend. Instead of pigging out when I got stressed, I chose not to overeat. Rethink*ing* with my affirmation mixed with rebound*ing* on my trampoline helped me change my old off-balance ways.

Rebounding was guiding me to change and become more balanced. I had found a tool for striking balance in my life. I rebounded before a date, before a big work assignment and even before I embarked on a creative project. I found myself smiling more, and I felt more relaxed and at peace! I felt more balanced and it began to play out in my decision-making. As a result, my life began to run more smoothly. Instead of constant dramas and mini-meltdowns, life was becoming serene, and I felt happier. I kept on jumping. I spent a minimum of ten minutes a day on the trampoline, reciting my affirmation, *"I love myself and I am balanced."* This daily commitment to balance informed all areas of my life. Whenever my addictive ego would pressure me to pick up a drink, eat too much or call a guy who was wrong for me, I would turn to this particular ~*ing* remedy. I'd recite my affirmation, jump on the trampoline, and in ten minutes bounce back to serenity.

Moreover, through daily repetition of this Balanc*ing* Equation, I began to perceive my life differently. I no longer saw myself as an over-eater, a co-dependent or an addictive, out-of-control person. I saw myself as grounded, balanced and at ease. My life had finally become manageable. I witnessed my relationships strengthen and my extreme behavior melt away. Another big side-effect was that I became much more cool and fun. As a result, I noticed that my friends wanted to hang with me more. I had become the "easygoing friend" instead of the "drama queen." In addition, I became more creative, which led me to revisit my childhood passion, painting. I set up an easel in my apartment and got to work. I liked the way it felt to honor my creative capacities and let my right brain do her thing. This transformation was truly a miracle.

Rebound*ing* has become a daily practice for me. My rebound*ing* adventure has led me to a more balanced life where I no longer need to seek outside stimuli to fill voids inside of me. And the truth is, once I began to live a more balanced life, I found that achieving balance leads to a life that is more satisfying and full. As a result, it's been a long time since I felt the sense of having a void that needed tending to. Plus, I have found a way to access serenity at will. Serenity is no longer a new-age buzzword for me; it is now my reality.

UNBALANCED BY PERFECTIONISM

While there are many forces that can come into play and cause life to be out of balance, in my own life and throughout my coaching experiences, I've noticed a common and frequent culprit: perfectionism. For a variety of reasons, our generation seems to be particularly susceptible to this trait. Many psychologists attribute the higher incidence of anxiety and alcoholism in Gen Y as compared to previous generations to this fact. Take my coaching client, Carolyn. At the age of eleven, Carolyn was diagnosed with diabetes. From that day forward, Carolyn felt an overwhelming fear of being imperfect due to her diagnosis. As a result, she spent the next twelve years avoiding the feeling of imperfection by striving to be perfect in all the areas of her life that she could "control." Chasing after perfection became her downfall.

Marinating in her unbalanced desire for perfection worked for a while, but as time went on it became more difficult. It was easy for her to be perfect in school or count her calories to maintain her perfect weight, but whenever there was a blip in the system, like an extra pound gained or an A- on an exam, Carolyn would go into a deep depression. This depressed feeling fed her need for perfection, making it even stronger. The feeling would ignite a fire under Carolyn to work harder, eat less and accomplish more. All of this perfecting and accomplishing was her way of avoiding the old feeling that dated back to that day in the doctor's office.

Carolyn finally hit bottom at age twenty-three. At the time she was working at a leading fashion magazine. In classic *Devil Wears Prada* style, she had become a slave to the industry. She often worked nights and weekends, chasing the high of perfection faster and harder than ever. The problem was that it was not possible for an entry-level hire to receive accolades in that kind of environment. Week after week she'd try to gain the approval of her boss, to no avail. Unable to achieve the impossible standard of perfection that she had set for herself, she crumbled.

In our first session together Carolyn and I identified her addiction to being perfect. She recognized the moment that her ego had taken over the wheel in the doctor's office twelve years earlier. Since then, she had led a life that was completely tilted toward achieving perfection—at any cost. Ready and willing to change and create a more balanced life for herself, she jumped right into the Balanc*ing* Equation. The first step was for her to recognize that even the ~*ing* work did not have to be done perfectly. I pumped her up with slogans like, "It's progress, not perfection!" and "It's cool to be 90 percent in motion, not 100 percent perfect." I encouraged her to jump outside her comfort zone and be a little sloppy. She started working with the affirmation: *I am willing to be imperfect.* Immediately, I put her on the trampoline while reciting that affirmation. When you bounce on a trampoline, you look and feel far from perfect or in control. That feeling of being out of control was great for Carolyn because she felt superuncomfortable.

It was my goal to push her out of her comfort zone and guide her through a new experience, one where she didn't get to have complete control. Specifically, I wanted her to physically experience the balance of being both in control and controlled by another force. It didn't take Carolyn long to make the connection. Within five minutes of rebounding she burst into tears as her entire body released, and she shouted joyfully, "I choose balance!" And she did. For thirty days she practiced the Balancing Equation. With each rebound, she gave up a little more control. Eventually, she let go of her perfectionist tendencies. And most exciting of all, she was able to add more balance into her life.

Her poor right brain, which had been silenced for so long, was finally allowed to assert itself. She was able to tap in to her creative side in a way she never had before, and discovered that she had a real talent for graphic design. As a result, she decided to pursue a career in graphic design. She quit her job, enrolled in a graphic design program, and now works in that industry.

By now I hope you've come to understand that becoming unbalanced can happen to anyone. Many in our generation have been trained to move so fast that we're never truly in touch with our feelings. If you're not moving fast, you're thinking fast. With Twitter, Facebook and Blackberry messenger, who has a chance to chill out? Life has become a constant search for outside stimuli with no roadmap inward. Well, enough already! I'm bringing serenity back! If you're ready to bounce back to serenity, test-drive my Balancing Equation. (Don't worry; you don't have to have a trampoline to do this one. I'll hook you up with some alternative activities if you don't.)

Before we begin the Balancing Equation, let's identify any behaviors that are causing you to be off-balance. To do that, answer the following questions: *Do you feel off-balance? Where are your addictive behaviors showing up in your life? Are you addicted to negative thoughts? Addicted to food? Sex? Alcohol? Work? Anything else? When you sense fear come up or when you become stressed, what is your immediate reaction? Do you run to the fridge? Pick up a drink? Hop on Facebook? Do you overthink things? Do you set unreasonably high expectations for yourself? If you don't achieve your personal expectations, do you beat yourself up?*

BALANCing EQUATION—
Thirty Days to Serenity

STEP ONE: Rethinking

Can you consider living in serenity? Wouldn't it feel good to wake up without anxiety, not concerned about what you ate the night before or if he's going to call you? Consider the idea of going through the day without obsessing over the same petty crap. This might be hard to fathom. It was for me. There was a point in time when I could not comprehend the word "serenity." But don't get discouraged. I guarantee you can make it happen. With a daily commitment to balance, you will be set free.

The first step to rethinking toward balance is to simply *choose* balance. The ego's addictive mind will resist balance at all costs. You may not realize this, but your number one addiction might be to thinking. You have more than 60,000 thoughts a day, and most of them are repeated obsessions that are totally let loose in your brain. The ego feeds off of these thoughts and will never let them go until you choose to take a stand. Additionally, the ego is armed with permission-giving thoughts. For example: "I'll start my diet tomorrow." "One drink won't hurt me." "I'll give this bad relationship one more shot." By giving yourself permission to act out, you keep yourself stuck in the negative behavior. You then become susceptible to peer pressure and the actions of others around you. In order to truly change your behavior, you must change your mind.

If you are ready to let go of your addictive patterns, make a fearless commitment to the following affirmation: *I commit to releasing my negative thought patterns. I choose balance and serenity.*

Breathe In—*I commit to releasing my negative thought patterns.*
Breathe Out—*I choose balance and serenity.*

STEP TWO: Rethinking + Moving

To reach a balanced life requires a mental and physical shift. Your body never truly feels aligned or grounded when your thoughts are constantly rocking the boat. When you consciously align your balanced affirmations with a rebounding exercise, you will experience a mind–body connection. This connection will inform your overall understanding of what it truly *feels* like to be balanced. It's in the *feeling* that the true transformation occurs.

If you happen to have access to a trampoline, get to rebounding! If you don't, here are a few alternative balanc*ing* activities that work just as well:

- Walk heel-to-toe. Place your heel just in front of the toes of your opposite foot each time you take a step. Your heel and toes should touch or almost touch. Walk around this way while you recite your affirmation.
- Stand on one foot. You can do this while looking in the mirror and stating your affirmation. Don't forget to alternate your feet.
- Practice standing up and sitting down without using your hands.
- Cross Crawl. This exercise is done by touching the right elbow to the left knee and then the left elbow to the right knee. When this exercise is performed in a slow and focused

manner, large areas of both brain hemispheres are activated at the same time. The cross crawl facilitates balanced nerve activation across the corpus callosum (that part in your brain that connects the right half to the left half). When done regularly, this exercise will work to connect the brain hemispheres bringing you to a more balanced state.

STEP THREE: Receiving (Meditating/~*ing write*)

Go to www.addmoreing.com and download for my balancing meditation, or just read below.

Begin by sitting straight up in a chair with your feet planted firmly on the ground. Envision that your feet are rooted into the earth. Your legs are like tree trunks that connect deeply into the earth. Your alignment is straight and you are balanced equally on either side. You are grounded and calm. Now listen to the voices in your mind. Allow them to pass through you. Don't react to any of the thoughts, just let them bounce in and out. These thoughts don't have to take you anywhere. They can just be with you. As you listen to these voices in your mind, allow yourself to breathe in the feelings they ignite. Allow these thoughts and feelings to flow through your body and out into the ground. Envision these toxic thoughts passing through you and releasing them for Mother Earth to recycle. Each thought can quickly pass through your legs and release as you choose.

No thought sways you. You remain grounded and balanced.

Breathe in serenity.

Breathe out peace.

Breathe in balance.

Breathe out joy.

Breathe in calm.

Breathe out faith.

Say these words: I am calm, I am balanced, I am serene.

~ing write

Following your meditation, allow your thoughts to flow freely onto the page; write whatever is in your mind after your meditation. Let the *~ing write* become a time to release your chaotic thoughts onto the page. Let your *inner guide* bring you back to equilibrium through the flow of each thought that passes through your pen. The paper can become your trampoline, where you rebound to a state of mental balance. Let the words release and allow your mind to rebound to a state of balance and serenity.

After practicing the Balanc*ing* Equation for the next thirty days, you'll begin to welcome a different perspective on life. This new perspective will guide you as you embark on the next chapter's journey. Welcome each perceptual shift as you take a close look into the Universal mirror.

CHAPTER FOUR

*Mirroring: The Good,
the Bad and the Ugly*

Perception is a mirror, not a fact. And what I look on is my state of mind, reflected outward.

The world is only in the mind of its maker. Do not believe it is outside of yourself.

—A Course in Miracles

Do you have a person in your life who just really gets under your skin? Someone whom you have to work yourself up to even be around, and then afterward you're reeling from the time spent with him or her because they managed to push every single one of your hot buttons. Maybe it's your boss, or an old friend that is still in your life even though you've outgrown her or him. Maybe it's your mom, dad, sister, brother or any other relative. The truth is, the very thing about that person that succeeds in pushing your buttons could very well be a mirror reflection of a similar deal in you.

And that's the reason the person gets so deeply under your skin. By this point, you're probably thinking: "There is no way that my nightmare of a boss or mother-in-law is providing a mirror into my own soul!" Believe me, I understand your confusion. But roll with me on this one. When I ran my PR business I had a client who drove me absolutely crazy, and if anyone had told me that his behavior could provide an opportunity for me to learn something about myself, I would have had my doubts. His motivating characteristic, which seemed to undercut everything I did, was that he was never satisfied. Every exchange with him felt like a cross-examination. It always seemed he was trying to one-up me or trip me up. It was pretty obvious once I got to know him that his competitive nature sprang from the fact that he was terribly insecure. He was the youngest of five brothers, was raised in a rough neighborhood, and, based on a childhood photo I once got a peek at, he was a bit of a runt growing up.

However, coming to an understanding of why he behaved this way did nothing to diffuse my frustration toward him. Even armed with my successful analysis, after spending time with him I'd be fuming and have difficulty letting go of my feelings of animosity and anger. It wasn't until about a year or so later, after I'd learned a method called "mirroring" and had actually become pretty good at it, that I came to understand why my exchanges with him tended to bother me so much: His obvious insecurity was a mirror to my own near-crippling insecurity that my work wasn't good enough. From the moment I signed contracts with him I began to feel like I was in way over my head. But once my own insecurities dissipated, my client's behavior completely stopped bothering me. I'd leave our monthly meeting and not think twice about a remark he'd made, whereas months before I'd have fumed for days. I only wish I had seen this reflection of my own insecurities sooner; it would have spared me several months of angst!

This experience reflects an often unrealized truth: the people and situations that tend to push our buttons the most are actually our best teachers. They serve as opportunities to uncover things about ourselves that are important for us to learn, so that we can either heal a chasm within ourselves or recognize something positive about ourselves in order to nurture it and allow it to blossom. This particular brand of self-reflection—the ability to learn different things about ourselves, the good, the bad and the ugly—is called "mirroring."

Mirroring teaches us that how we experience relationships and situations in our lives is often a direct reflection of how we feel internally. For example, if you believe in yourself, others will believe in you. If you say hurtful things to yourself, others' comments will hurt you—comments that often have no hurtful intention behind them. If you respect yourself, others will respect you. According to the *Course*, we come across our feelings about ourselves in others. Often, when we are upset with others, it is because we are seeing in them what we don't like about ourselves. The miracle comes when we stop blaming others for our unhappiness and are willing to look inward for healing. In this chapter we'll further explore the concept of mirroring, focusing on how the ~*ing* Equation can actually help draw out the self-reflective opportunities that exist within life's challenging people and experiences.

RELATIONSHIPS IN THE MIRROR

While anyone you meet at any time can act as a self-reflective mirror, most often it's those people who play important roles in our lives that give us the best opportunity to learn about ourselves. Why? Two reasons. One, we spend more time with them, and it's through time and shared experiences that you can truly get to know someone layer by layer. In addition, it's the people who know us best who can really press our hot buttons. And it's through a strong reaction to something, either a person or an event, that we can catch a glimpse into the mirror and thus put the mirroring exercise to work. It's the strong feeling—whether it's frustration at your mom for always nagging you about your career, or anger at a boss for his constant criticism, or even annoyance at a friend for always needing to be the center of attention—that helps you figure out what the person or situation can teach you about yourself.

Relationships are complicated, and let's face it, we all have people in our lives who get under our skin and push our buttons.

The great thing about mirroring is that it not only helps you accept these folks, it allows you to turn the tables on any angst you might be suffering in those relationships. Ultimately, you'll be able to able to turn a situation that was once frustrating into a learning experience that will help you live a more self-aware life.

REPRESSED FEELINGS IN THE MIRROR

One of the biggest benefits of mirroring is that it is a way to uncover repressed feelings that you might not even realize exist in your subconscious. Emily, a twenty-eight-year-old client of mine, lost her job in the fall of 2008. As a result of her layoff she was unable to afford her apartment, so she had to move back in with her parents. Although she knew the move wasn't permanent, she found living at home to be unbearable. Emily struggled to figure out what to do with her life. Indeed, Emily hadn't just lost her job, she had lost her career. Her work as an event planner was hard to come by in this economic climate, or so said the voice in her head. The truth underneath that thought was that she had an inner desire to do something different. Her dream was to move to Africa and be of service to a community in need. For years she had longed to use her coordinating skills to help the world in a philanthropic way. However, her fear of the unknown was blocking her from taking action to make this dream a reality. When she mentioned her desires to her parents, they immediately disapproved and were totally unsupportive. In fact, they threatened to stop helping her financially unless she committed to finding another event-planning job in the United States.

Meanwhile, in an effort to help her find some clarity and get a hit of positivity, Emily's friend suggested she attend one of my lectures. My topic that night happened to be mirroring. To illustrate how mirroring works, I asked the audience to identify mirrors in their relationships and life circumstances. To find their mirrors, I suggested they consider people or situations that made them really uncomfortable in some way. Immediately, Emily raised her hand. She told us about how her parents disapproved of her desire to move to Africa and how they put her down for even considering it. Filled with sadness and stuck in the role of the victim, Emily asked me, "How could this situation possibly be a mirror for me? My parents are totally out of line. They don't believe I'm worthy of going to Africa to help people." I responded, "Do *you* believe you're worthy?"

As she considered my question, tears rolled down her face. She replied, "I guess not." By offering Emily the opportunity to see her reflection in the mirror of her parents' resistance, I helped her to understand it better. Her parents' lack of belief in her ability to apply her skills mirrored her own lack of confidence in herself. Unconsciously, Emily's parents felt her insecurity; therefore, they too were fearful of her decision to go to Africa. Had she approached them with confidence, they would have reacted differently, regardless of their own agenda. If her energy was confident, they too would have felt confident. A month later, this proved to be the case. Emily did major research into nonprofit job opportunities available to her in Africa. She began applying, and once she was hired for a position, she mapped out her move and felt powerfully committed to her plan. As a result, she was much more confident about her decision. When she revisited the topic with her parents, she presented her plan to them with ease and self-assurance. As a result, their energy and attitude totally shifted. Now they mirrored her confidence.

When you use the mirroring process in your relationships, the key is to check in with how the people in your life you have difficulties with are making you feel about yourself. Then ask your *inner guide* to give you greater insight into what unhealed perceptions live underneath the feelings. This process will result in stronger, more amicable relationships because you'll no longer harbor resentment toward others. As a result, you can redirect that energy toward cleaning up your feelings and creating a healthier reflection in the mirror.

SHORTCOMINGS IN THE MIRROR

Another great thing about mirroring is that it allows us to take a look at our own shortcomings. Indeed, often the very qualities that we react strongly to in others are qualities that reside within ourselves.

With this new awareness, I challenge you to pay attention when you're pointing the finger at others. Use your unpleasant feelings as triggers for you to pivot and look inward. These moments are opportunities for you to gaze into the Universal mirror and figure out what funky stuff is lingering inside you. Maybe an old friend you've outgrown gets on your nerves every time you see her because she is always stirring up drama, and every time she hangs out with you and your circle of friends, she starts a fight.

So where's the reflection of you in this? Well, maybe you didn't get enough attention in your clique of friends in school. Maybe you were shyer than others, and although you craved attention, the spotlight fell on those who were more outgoing. Now you can't help but feel like the kid who is still trying to be heard when your drama queen friend is around to soak up everyone's attention— even if it is negative attention she's getting. If you're ready to take responsibility for the reflection in your mirror, I encourage you to stop pointing at others and start looking inward. Whenever you find yourself putting others down or focusing on their faults, this is a sure sign that you're not diggin' what you've got goin' on in you. People who love to point out the faults in others are really just super scared to see the faults in themselves.

THE POSITIVES IN THE MIRROR

Mirrors don't just reflect the things we need to change. They also reflect the beauty within us. The beauty you see in the world is the beauty you see in yourself. For example, I once watched my friend's band perform in the park. I was so moved by the band's happiness on the stage and the beautiful music that I started to cry. I realized that the joy I felt while watching the band was a reflection of the joy I feel inside. Appreciating the greatness in others is a beautiful mirror to appreciate the greatness you feel internally.

THE MIRROR*ing* EQUATION

The Mirror*ing* Equation will guide you to interpret what the Universe reflects back to you. If you take this tool seriously, you will uncover hidden aspects of yourself that you may have been afraid to see. One of the key tools for using the mirror as a guide is to never overanalyze your reflections. That's why we'll begin the Equation with the movement step—which in this case will be walk*ing*—rather than the usual rethink*ing* step. I'll ask you to apply the literal action of walking to the figurative action of walking away from whatever situation may have ignited negative feelings in you from the mirroring process. In your walk, you will reflect on your reactions to the moments of self-awareness you are dealing with.

This step is followed by a meditation where I'll lead you to check in with your ~*ing* for further feedback on what you've learned from your recent mirroring process. To foster a deeper look into the mirror, you'll follow your meditation with an ~*ing write* where even more inner truth and self-reflection can come through on the page. Finally, you will hit the rethink*ing* step, where I'll offer you several tools for applying the mirroring process in your life.

Before you begin the Mirror*ing* Equation, ask yourself the following questions: *Do you often feel defensive, agitated or frustrated in response to others? Are there certain people who can really push your buttons?*

THE MIRROR*ing* EQUATION
Thirty Days of Reflecting

STEP ONE: Mov*ing* ⸱
As soon as possible after you have used the mirroring process to figure out how someone else's behavior is a reflection of something deep within yourself—either a shortcoming or a repressed emotion—I ask that you take your ego for a walk.

Walk away from the situation that has triggered your mirror. Take yourself on a fifteen-minute walk and allow your mind to flow. Let your thoughts and feelings move through you with each step. Welcome each thought. Don't push them away or judge them, just listen. The *Course* teaches us that the ego speaks first and loudest. Therefore, recognize that your initial thoughts might be of the ego. Simply allow them to pass with each step you take. Walk to a nearby park, ocean, bench or stoop where you feel comfortable. Then sit for a five-minute meditation.

Step Two: Receiving (Meditating/~*ing write*)

Gently close your eyes. Take a deep breath in through your nose and out through your mouth. Let yourself settle into your surroundings. Think about the person or situation that has mirrored your inner emotion. Say out loud to the Universe, "Please help me understand this mirror. What do I need to learn here?" Then sit for five minutes and listen to your *inner guidance*. Stay open to the message. It may come in the form of a feeling or a thought. Sense your feelings in the moment. Breathe and receive. Keep in mind that you may not get an answer right away. Be patient and know that your intuition can speak to you at any time of day. Stay open to the answers.

~*ing write*

Immediately following your meditation, flow right into your ~*ing write*. Allow your truthful *inner voice* to come through in your writing. Relax your mind and let your thoughts be guided by your ~*ing*. Let your feelings guide you as you write. Reflect on how you've been reacting to whatever you learned from the mirroring process. For instance, if what you learned about yourself from your mother's constant nagging about how you don't have a boyfriend is that you are terrified that you will never fall in love, write about how that makes you feel. If what you learned from your friend who bugs you because she's a terrible gossip is that you yourself love to gossip because putting other people down makes you feel better about yourself, write about how *that* makes you feel. Don't judge, just witness. Remember that the mirror is not an opportunity to beat yourself up, but instead is a chance to grow. Each mirror offers you deeper self-awareness.

STEP THREE: Rethinking

Now that you have had time to really think about what you learned about yourself from the mirroring technique, it's time to figure out how you're going to make a change. For instance, keeping with the two examples I've used throughout the Equation, if you discovered that you secretly love to gossip about others, it's time to accept that you're ready to address that behavior. The same applies if you discovered a repressed emotion, such as your fear of never falling in love: you can choose to flip the switch on that fear. When you've recognized what behavior you need to address, write it down. For instance, you might write, "I am going to make a conscious effort to NOT gossip about others." Or, "I'm going to stop wasting energy on being afraid that I'll never fall in love and instead apply that energy to getting out into the world and experiencing life." To help facilitate further change, you can flip back a few pages and apply one of these issues to your Feeling, Forgiving or Balancing Equations.

Enjoy using your mirror as a tool for internal growth and an honest appraisal of yourself. Remember that each mirror is a beautiful opportunity to look inward and clear more space to receive *inner guidance.* "Clean but the mirror and the message shines forth," says *A Course in Miracles.*

Your thirty-day Mirroring practice will come in handy when practicing the next chapter's Equation. In chapter five I'll guide you toward releasing the ego's illusions in romantic relationships. Your newfound understanding of how to use the mirror will be a useful tool when taking a closer look at how you approach relationships.

CHAPTER FIVE

Releasing:
Romantic Illusions

Your task is not to seek for love, but merely to seek and find all of the barriers within yourself that you have built against it.

Idols are limits. They are the belief that there are forms that will bring happiness . . . Decide for idols and you ask for loss.

—A Course in Miracles

Michelle had it goin' on! She had a great job, great friends, a healthy perception of herself and lots of cool hobbies. In her spare time she enjoyed dance classes, reading fiction and visiting museums. Her life was easy, breezy and full of inspiration. Then she met Aaron. The moment they met, their brains became flooded with hormones. Because Michelle hadn't had much experience with romance, she was overwhelmed by the feelings that came over her. She felt as though she was glowing from the inside out. Her heart was beating faster and her body felt numb, as if she were wrapped in a love burrito. They were vibing, to say the least. Within a week they had spun into a serious relationship.

By the second month of their romance, Michelle's friends Samantha and Lila started to speak up about the changes they'd noticed in her. "You never hang out with us anymore." "You seem so anxious all the time." "What happened to our happy friend?" What had happened was that Michelle's newfound romance had sucked her into an ego tornado. In the beginning of the relationship, the couple became super-obsessed with each other, and by the second month they had completely lost track of their own lives. To make matters worse, Michelle's relationship with Aaron ignited insecurities she hadn't even realized that she had.

Her ego went crazy creating tons of delusional fears that Michelle had never faced before. As a result of her ego's romantic illusions, she wound up losing track of the awesomeness of her life. She began to perceive Aaron as her only source of happiness, and totally neglected all of the relationships she'd had in her life before they met. She idolized him and only felt truly complete when they were together.

Michelle's best friend, Samantha, resented her friend's relationship with Aaron. Her anger toward their relationship was a perfect mirror for her own inner anger. Samantha was angry at herself for not having the courage to fall in love. Because her father had left her family when she was a child, she lived in fear of men leaving. Inevitably, she was unable to truly experience romantic love as a result of her ego's control.

Lila, on the other hand, experienced a different kind of envy when Michelle became involved with Aaron. She was filled with resentment over losing her friend to a guy. To make matters worse, she was jealous of Michelle for having a boyfriend. Lila had put an insane amount of emphasis on the importance of having a boyfriend. This was the result of the pressure her mother put on her to get married. Therefore, watching her friend become involved in a relationship raised the level of fear she had that she wasn't good enough without a boyfriend.

I'm confident that you can personally relate to either Michelle, Samantha or Lila's situations, or know someone who has experienced the ego's antics around romance. When the ego strikes romantic relationships, all love is thrown out the window. Remember that the *Course* refers to the ego as "Quite literally a fearful thought." Therefore, when ego enters a romantic relationship (or simply one's perception of a romantic relationship), all hell breaks loose. As you may already know, this is a particular area of life that can be overwhelmingly difficult. Romance is where the ego can really take you down.

I've totally been in a place similar to all three of these ladies. As a result of dealing with many of my ego's romantic tragedies, I finally wised up and decided it was time to release my romantic illusions. In this chapter, I'm going to give you a healthy dose of the lessons I learned when I slowly but surely did. Thanks to the *Course*, dating and relationships have become much more fun for me,and way easier to navigate. So, in this chapter, I will share with you exactly how the *Course* completely changed my perceptions of dating and relationships. First I'll explain how the ego acts up in romantic relationships. Then I'll give you a heads-up on how the ego blocks your ~*ing* when it comes to romance. Next I'll take you through the payoff of applying the ~*ing* Equation in your effort to recover from the havoc the ego wreaks on the relationship front. By sharing what I've learned, I hope to simplify for you an area of life that is often perceived as super complicated.

THE UNROMANTIC EGO

The ego is to blame for the complexity of relationships. The unromantic ego is really just a screwed up delusion based on dwelling in the past and fear of the future. Typically, people enter into a romantic relationship lugging their past with them. I've watched normal, balanced people turn into complete freaks as a result of the ego's romantic delusions. In fact, I was one of them.

For instance, the ego's voice often tells you that you're not good enough for your partner, or that he or she isn't good enough for you. Or your ego tells you that your happiness lies in the arms of another person. Often the ego will mirror the behavior of one or both of your parents. For example, if you grew up with a submissive mother, you may follow in her footsteps. Or if your father put you down, you may choose a partner who also puts you down. The behaviors we picked up from our parents directly affect our present relationships. Unfortunately, the past situations that the ego re-creates always get the best of any romance.

Additionally, the ego causes trouble in romantic relationships by using your fears from the past to totally freak you out in the present. If your previous boyfriend cheated on you, you likely will have trust issues with your current boyfriend, even though he's done nothing to cause you to distrust him. To make matters worse, the ego keeps you from being authentic for fear of not being cool. For instance, Lara spent over a year in a relationship with Dan pretending to like sports, house music and the beach in order to make him think she was cool. Meanwhile, Dan never got a chance to see what Lara's true interests were. As a result of never seeing the real her, he broke up with her because he felt she really didn't bring much to the relationship, and he was looking to learn more from a partner. Lara's ego caused her to deny her inner truth, which took her down a delusional path that resulted in her losing a relationship.

Finally, the ego screams crazy talk to the world, like "Men love bitches" and "Women are difficult." These so-called "facts" are straight-up garbage ideas that must be dispelled. If you're ready to release all of the romantic illusions that have been sabotaging your romantic relationships, arm yourself with the following tools and take them with you on a thirty-day releasing journey.

HOW THE UNROMANTIC EGO BLOCKS YOUR ~*ing*

Special Relationships

A big no-no in romance is casting your partner as an idol. Lessons from the *Course* have taught me to "see beyond all idols." When you idolize a romantic partner, you turn them into your only source of happiness. Without them you feel incomplete. This is a nightmare. The *Course* teaches, "It is never the idol that you want, but what you think it offers you." If you depend on one specific person for all your happiness, you're totally screwed. This is much like what ultimately ended up happening to Michelle and Aaron. Michelle consistently put her relationship before her friendships, career and personal life. Michelle made Aaron her idol and denied her ~*ing*, seeking all of her guidance and love from him.

This is what the *Course* refers to as the ego's "special relationship." In actuality, the "special relationship" isn't all that special. In fact, it separates you from your *inner guidance* because it makes you believe that your "salvation" (happiness) is outside of you and in the arms of your significant other. The word "special" implies "different," which to the ego means "better than." When you make your significant other "special," he or she becomes better than your friends, better than your career, better than your family and definitely better than you. It is said in the *Course* that, "The special love relationship is the ego's chief weapon for keeping you from Heaven." (When the *Course* speaks of Heaven, it means the rockin' way of living fearless, happy and connected to your ~*ing* at all times.)

Moreover, the "special relationship" is two incomplete people who have come together to fill each other's voids. The "special relationship" is one person's emptiness and insecurity filling up the other person's. One person's need to be completed fills the other person's need to be validated. Like in Lila's case, where she felt she had to have a boyfriend in order to feel complete. Then she met Matt. He was an insecure guy who never felt good enough unless he had a girl on his arm. Lila's incompleteness was the perfect void filler for Matt's incompleteness. As a result, they became totally obsessed and made idols of each other. Their relationship continued this way for a while until Lila decided she was ready to find other fulfillments outside of her relationship with Matt. Toward that end, she secured a new job, made new friends and started hitting the gym.

These new pursuits filled her up on the inside, and as a result, she no longer needed Matt to fill a void. Matt's unhealed insecurity soon became totally unattractive to Lila. And for his part, Matt began to resent Lila for her new passions. Finally, Lila broke up with Matt, leaving him alone with his feelings of being incomplete. This is one of the many unhealthy outcomes of "special relationships."

The "special relationship" is always on shaky ground. This "special" person has been placed on such a high pedestal that if he or she makes the slightest mistake, you will fall apart as a result of feeling incomplete. The *Course* reiterates my point with this quote: "Behind the search for every idol lies the yearning for completion." The ~*ing* girl translation: When you idolize your partner, that implies that you think you are incomplete without them. Because you don't feel whole on your own, you *yearn for completion* in another person. It's kinda like that bogus line in *Jerry McGuire* when he says, "You complete me." Sorry to break it to you, but no relationship can *ever* complete you. The reality is that you don't have to look that far to feel complete.

All the awesomeness you desire already lives inside of you! I know you might be thinking, "Oh no, here she goes with that *all the love you need is inside of you* crap." Well, ya know what? I am going there! That is *exactly* what I'm saying. I am saying that YOU are completely whole, filled with an infinite amount of love that no relationship could possibly compare to. These may just be words to you today, but I am proud to testify to this greater source of love. The *Course* asserts: "You have so little faith in yourself because you are unwilling to accept the fact that perfect love is in you, and so you seek without for what you cannot find within." When you stop seeking happiness from the outside and turn to ~*ing* for self-love, you will learn to stop searching for "special relationships." This chapter's ~*ing* Equation, aka the Releas*ing* Equation, equips you with tools that will guide you to see the greatness that lives inside of you.

Clutching and Controlling

Sally showed up to her coaching session with me complaining that she felt alone, that her friends and boyfriend were not showing up for her. She complained that her boyfriend, who was studying in Europe, was not replying to her e-mails, her friends were not attending her social events and her sister wasn't returning her phone calls. She felt unheard and ignored by the world.

The backstory on Sally is that these feelings of being ignored stem from her childhood. As a little girl she could never get the proper attention from her father, who was clinically depressed and emotionally unable to give her the attention she craved. Sally came to me a year ago, filled with anger toward her father. As a result of this anger, she has replayed the tensions she has in her relationship with her father in all of her romantic relationships and friendships for the past fifteen years. Furthermore, she developed a tendency to control, manipulate, push and scream in order to get people to respond to her.

Her outer rage is her kneejerk response mirroring her un-healed anger toward her father. I explained to Sally that her friends are not her father, and that if she continued to equate happiness with attention from others she would be screwed. I continued to teach her that the reason her friends were not responding to her was because behind every request was a manipulative expectation. With each request, she was serving them her past on a platter. Fol-lowing the suggestion of the Sufi poet Rumi, I encouraged her to "stop serving them your pain." Further, I explained that we are truly heard by others only when we ask without expectation.

There are two major lessons to be learned from Sally's story. The first is that you'll get back the energy you give out. If you serve people manipulative, controlling energy, they will run. I explained to Sally that her issue wasn't *what* she was asking for, but *how* she was asking. Regardless of her kind tone of voice, the controlling energy behind the request was what sent everyone running. I ex-plained that her boyfriend could even feel her controlling energy through the Internet.

All efforts to clutch and smother the people in our lives in order to fill our own need for love and attention inevitably end up working against those relationships. So what can you do to change this? One word: Release.

THE LESSONS

Lesson Number One: Your Romantic Partner Is Not Your Only Light Switch
The ego makes you believe that the only way you can experi-ence sparks is through romantic love. To help you see this dif-ferently, the *Course's* philosophy is that you should strive to make

your romantic relationships more brotherly and your brotherly re-lationships more romantic. The term "brotherly" simply means "friendship." The *Course* teaches that you should stop idolizing your lover and bring an equal perception of love to everyone in your life. When you take the emphasis off of that one person, they are no longer so "special."

A powerful example of this was shared in one of my round-table group coaching sessions. Alexandra shared a powerful story of how the "specialness" she had created in her romantic rela-tionships became clear to her when she went to a concert with some friends. One of her girlfriends was arriving a little late. Throughout the first set, Alexandra didn't even notice that her friend wasn't there yet. When she finally looked at her watch, she realized that her friend was over an hour late. She sent her a sweet text saying, "I hope the traffic isn't too bad. Wish you were here!" Her friend arrived for the second half of the show and they had a great time.

Later that night Alexandra reflected on the evening. She envi-sioned how differently she would have handled that situation if she had been waiting for a date rather than her friend. Had her date ar-rived over an hour later due to traffic, she would have totally flipped out. There was no way she would have enjoyed the show and no way she would have released her anger by the time he arrived. This situation was a clear indication that Alexandra placed her roman-tic relationships in a separate (higher) category than her friend-ships. It was super cool that she identified this so clearly and saw how powerful her ego could be. The ego loves to make romance scary and separate from all the other relationships in your life.

Start to see your lovers or dates as friends. Imagine how cool it would be if you could be 100 percent relaxed and authentic on a date! Try it out. Lighten up your romantic relationships by viewing your partner as a friend. Start by simply being yourself, and act as if you're out with your friends. It may be tough at first, but it works. Relax and just be you. Your authentic truth is sexy. So stop pretending and start being. Most anyone can sniff bullshit a mile away. Be yourself!

On the other hand, make your friendships more romantic. I have been known to rave about the fiery passion I have on a nightly basis. This passion comes from the groups of women I coach. The love and richness in these groups is indescribable. When I'm working with my groups I feel the high of being in love. And that's because I am! I am *in love* with each woman in the room. I'm in love with the energy we create as a group and with the healing that occurs. The energy in the room fills my heart as if a boyfriend had professed his love for the first time. Every woman in the groups can testify to this experience.

Therefore, I've put them to the test. I asked them to begin shifting their perceptions about special relationships by witnessing all the romance that is already around them within their friendships. They came back to the group with the most incredible stories of love in their friendships. For example, Erica went to LA to visit a girlfriend and wound up spending the entire week wrapped with love. This love came from their shared passion for spirituality. The two women exulted in their connection and didn't want to leave each other's side. "It felt like falling in love," said Erica. When you have passion, fire and romance in your friendships, why do you need to grasp for it in a lover? Sure, you can have both—but why not let your friendships be equally as passionate? Let romance have no boundaries. Let passionate love surface in *all* of your relationships.

The concept that your lover isn't your only light switch might be tough to grasp. This is not what you've been trained to believe. You've been brought up with fairy tales of Prince Charming and the knight in shining armor. As beautiful as all that might sound, it really did a number on you. These fairy tales totally back up the ego's perception of "special love." I'm not here to burst your bubble; I'm just here to expand it.

Lesson Number Two: Relationships Are Assignments

Have you been repeating the same patterns in every romantic relationship? Do you replay the same behavior and continue to receive the same results? The reason for this is that all relationships are assignments, because, as the *Course* teaches us, the obstacles we face in all relationships are opportunities for optimal growth. The Universe brings together those individuals who have the greatest capacity for learning and healing.

I'll use my friend Gina as an example of how all relationships are assignments. Gina spent a year in a relationship with Will. By the end of the year, she was fed up with his noncommittal attitude. She was ready to get married, but unfortunately, he wasn't in the same mind-set. Rather than following her ego, Gina listened to her *inner guide*. The voice inside her said, "Forgive him and release him; he's doing the best he can." She followed the voice of her *inner guide* and broke up with Will in a powerfully peaceful way. This experience taught her the lesson of forgiveness. Since she forgave him and released him, she was able to remain his friend even though the breakup was painful. Having had an optimal learning experience with Will, she was ready for another assignment.

Gina soon met a man named Garret who shared her goal of marriage. Gina and Garret spent seven months in a lovely relationship where Gina learned two major lessons and practiced new behavior. She learned how to receive and to honor her needs. At the end of the seventh month, Garret unexpectedly broke up with

Gina. To Gina's surprise, she wasn't very disappointed. She knew that though this sweet relationship hadn't lasted long, it had provided her maximal learning opportunities. The *Course* teaches that when the opportunities to learn are over, the relationship will be replaced by something better (and new opportunities for learning). That's exactly what happened to Gina. Within two weeks she reconnected with Will. In the time they'd spent apart, he'd experienced many optimal learning opportunities himself. In his case, his learning experiences had transpired in his relationship with himself. He had learned to truly love himself, and therefore realized he was ready to properly love Gina.

As a result of their shared healing, they were ready to embark on a new journey. They'd transformed their "special" relationship into a healthy, balanced one by showing up for their individual assignments. Gina and Will no longer needed to fill each other's voids and instead were just happy to share their light with one another. After they had worked through their individual assignments, the Universe brought them back together.

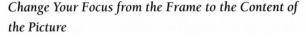

THE SHIFT

Change Your Focus from the Frame to the Content of the Picture

Another payoff of the Releas*ing* Equation is that you begin to focus on the content of the relationship rather than the frame of what it looks like on the outside. The *Course* positions the "special relationship" as a picture frame that holds up "important" worldly desires—how much money he makes, his religion, his body type, etc. Alternatively, the *holy* relationship is based on the content of the picture rather than the frame. When you're focused on the content rather than the frame, you could care less about how much money he makes, and be more concerned with how he makes you *feel*. By shifting your focus from the frame to the content, you can begin to experience the person's truth. This is when you are truly *vibing*. It is in releasing the ego's worldly frame that you can see your partner for his true essence—love.

The Holy Instant

Romantic relationships have always tripped me up. For years I'd recreate the same illusions in all my romances. I had one relationship in particular where my ego always got the best of me. I spent a full year being angry, judgmental and stuck in the past. I was defensive and unforgiving. I tried using my mirror to see these reflections as guides to my own issues, but my ego kept me pointing the finger at my boyfriend. This egoic pattern continued up until one Fourth of July vacation weekend. My ego spent the entire weekend telling me fearful stories about my relationship. By the second day of our vacation I was fed up with my ego's chatter.

So before we went out to see the fireworks, I decided to sit in a meditation and turn to my *inner guide* for some help. As I sat, I let my ~*ing* do her thing. I released my thoughts to the Universe and listened to the voice of my *inner guide*. At the beginning of my meditation I said out loud, "I surrender my anger toward my boyfriend and I choose to forgive him. Help me see him differently." Within seconds I felt my angst soften and my ~*ing* take the lead. My boyfriend entered into my meditation. I saw him clearly before me. We stood across from one another. Soon his body began to change. Beams of white light poured through him, and his bodily form disappeared. Even though I couldn't see his body, I had a sense that he was still with me. I felt an overwhelming feeling of relief. I was wrapped with love.

In that moment I was able to truly forgive him for the lies my ego had placed on him and see him as an equal rather than someone "special." In seeing his innocence, I felt as though we were one connected energy of white sparkling light. This was way better than any Fourth of July fireworks! This was a "holy instant."

The holy instant can occur any moment that you choose to bring your fears to your ~ing for healing. Your ~ing can heal as much as you will offer it. In the holy instant, your ~ing leads you to undo the illusions of your ego through forgiveness. In my case, this love shined through when I was able to see my boyfriend as an equal rather than "special" and separate from me. In that instant I was able to release my fears and anger and see him for his true essence.

As a result, I was filled with a sense of peace. The *Course* writes, "In the holy instant, no-one is special, for your personal needs intrude on no-one, to make them different. Without the values from the past you would see them all the same, and like yourself. Nor would you see any separation between yourself and them. In the holy instant, you see, in each relationship, what it will be, when you perceive only the present."

The Holy Relationship

There is a way of being in relationships that allows you to choose to perceive most everything with loving lenses upon first glance. This is what the *Course* calls the "holy relationship." Below I will walk you through the steps of the Releas*ing* Equation, which will help you to release your romantic illusions. Once you have succeeded in letting these illusions go, you will be rewarded with the ability to start getting closer to creating holy relationships.

A holy relationship starts with a different premise. That premise is: Each one has looked within and seen no lack. Accepting his completion, he would extend it by joining with another, whole as himself. This text from the *Course* describes the holy relationship as two whole, healed individuals who join together in love rather than fear. The holy relationship happens for those who have shown up for their assignments and followed their ~*ing*. As a result of each party's personal wholeness, they no longer need to make their partner an idol. In the holy relationship the participants perceive each other as equals. The *Course* states: "The holiness in you belongs to him. And by your seeing it in him, returns to you." This explains that the light inside these two whole individuals mirrors one another. The light they see in their love is their own inner light reflected back to them. In the holy relationship, the other person doesn't complete you, but instead enjoys your wholeness with you.

APPLYING THE ~*ing* EQUATION TO RELATIONSHIPS

The Releas*ing* Equation will guide you to transform your romantic delusions of "special love" into holy perceptions. The first step of the equation, the rethink*ing* step, will guide you to find light in other areas of your life besides your romantic partner. In addition, the Equation asks that you take inventory of how you've been perceiving romance and provides you with tools for rethink*ing* any negative perceptions. Then, in the mov*ing* section of the Equation, you'll be introduced to some of the best light-igniting physical activities I've ever ~*inged* with. These light-igniting activities will present you with an outlet for becoming your own light switch.

By accessing more light in yourself, you will be guided to relieve yourself of any "special relationships" you've created. (You will relieve them too.) Next, the Equation arms you with a series of meditations that I've strategically created for releas*ing* romantic il-lusions. These meditations have saved me from many unnecessary meltdowns. To fully receive your *inner guidance*, you will follow the meditation and *~ing write* a release letter to yourself that will put you on the road toward new behavior. This letter will be a sacred contract you make with yourself and the Universe to commit to change. It will also act as an ongoing reminder for how your ego can get the best of you when it comes to romantic love.

The Releas*ing* Equation will provide you with the tools for honoring your *~ing* in each relationship you're in so that you can show up for all the assignments the relationship has in store for you. Practicing the Releas*ing* Equation in every romantic assign-ment will guide you toward experiencing what the *Course* calls "holy love."

Upon beginning the Releas*ing* Equation, look closely at your patterns in romantic relationships. Ask yourself the following ques-tions: *Do you get tripped up over romance? Do you find yourself replaying the same patterns over and over in each relationship? Are you stuck in fear when it comes to romance?*

THE RELEAS*ing* EQUATION
Thirty Days to Releas*ing* Your Romantic Illusions

STEP ONE: Rethink*ing*
To overcome your ego's misconceptions of romance, you must begin by changing your mind. First I ask that you take a close look at your ego's patterns in romantic relationships. Then I'll guide you to see things differently by shifting your focus from the frame to the picture. Next you'll be led to find light in other areas of your

life besides your romantic partner. Finally, you'll learn ways to turn on your own light switches rather than rely on your partner for your only source of light.

Take a Look at Your Ego's Patterns in Romantic Relationships:

- Make a list of your meaningful romantic relationships, past and present.
- ~*Ing write* the "story" of each one. How did it start? What was the dynamic? How did it end? What's it like today?
- Get clear about the nasty stories your ego's been telling you about romantic love.

Shift Your Focus from the Frame to the Picture

Make a list of how your partner makes you *feel* joy. If you are single, make a list of how you want a partner to make you *feel* joy. By acknowledging how your partner makes you want to feel within, you take the emphasis off of all the stuff on the surface, such as how much money he makes, what his degree is in, etc.; all this stuff is the frame. How he makes you *feel* is the content. Remember, the content of a relationship is what truly matters. The frame can't hold up forever.

Access Other Sources of Light

- Make a list of the light in other areas of your life (playing with your pet, exercising, listening to music, writing, etc.).
- Spot-check the romance, passion and sparks that exist within your friendships.
- Make a list of where love effortlessly shines. Is there love in your family relationships and friendships? Is it in your

books? Is it in a creative project? It might even come in the form of a pet. Recognizing the love around you is a reflection of the love that's in you.

Hang Out in the Light

Whenever your ego tries to convince you that love only comes in the form of a romantic partner, prove it wrong. Do this by immediately flipping on one of your other light switches. For instance, listen to songs that ignite your spirit. Or take your dog for a walk. For the next thirty days, engage daily in at least one of the areas of your life that shine light on you (other than romance).

Go on a Date with Yourself

Take yourself somewhere you might not go by yourself. Make yourself a picnic in the park. Go to a museum. Enjoy a romantic comedy. Find romance in being with yourself.

STEP TWO: Rethinking + Moving

There is a specific aerobic workout that ignites your inner light like no other. It's called intenSati. Founded by *~ing* guru Patricia Moreno, this workout combines a hardcore cardio dance workout with positive affirmations. *Inten* means "intention," and *Sati* means "mindfulness." The combination of powerful movement and positive affirmations creates miraculous shifts in your core and blasts your inner light through you. If I'm ever in a foul mood or over-thinking some ego B.S., I can hop into an intenSati class and everything will shift within the hour. And the best part is that it is accessible to you at home via Patricia's numerous DVDs (www. addmoreing.com).

Any activity that gets your body into a positive flow will have the power to ignite your *inner light*. In addition to intenSati, I suggest taking classes in African and Bollywood dance or Brazilian capoeira (an ~*ing* girl fave!).

STEP THREE: Receiving (Mediating/~*ing write*)

Meditation was my primary tool for transforming my romantic illusions into loving reality. As a result, I've created meditations that are specific to releasing the ego's fear in relationships. The goal of these meditations is to allow your ~*ing* to surface the truthful feelings that dwell underneath the ego's fear. Each time you bring your fears to your *inner guide* through meditation, you release your ego and love can truly surface.

Release Meditation

Meditation leads you to freedom from the ego's "special relationship." The *Course* states: "Release yourself and release others." Set them free by releasing them on a daily basis. This often requires the "F" word. It is highly possible that you have listened to your ego's false stories about your partner and identified them as reality. Forgive your partner through your meditation. Remember that it is in forgiving that *you* are released. When you release your lover, you let him be who he needs to be, and in the midst of forgiveness you can truly see him for who he really is. This is beautiful work that can really change your relationships for the rest of your life. When the illusion lifts, you can also see the relationship for its truth. This work could also lead to a peaceful breakup. Forgiveness is your guide to a lovingly aligned relationship. It provides the clarity and love you need to make honest decisions that are based on your *inner guidance* rather than your ego. This tool sets you both free. Let go of the outcome and enjoy the freedom.

Download the meditation off www.addmoreing.com, or read below:

Take a deep breath in through your nose and breathe out through your mouth.

Hold a vision of your lover in your mind.

See him standing before you.

Smile as you welcome in his vision.

Take a deep breath in and recite in your mind—*I forgive you.*

Breathe out—*I release you.*

Breathe in—*I accept you.*

Breathe out—*The light in you reflects the light in me.*

We share this light.

Envision a ball of white light forming inside your heart.

On the exhale, send light from your heart to his heart.

This light represents your love and your true connection.

On the inhale, call the light from his heart back into your heart.

Hold the vision of this shared light and continue to inhale the light and exhale the light back to him.

See a beautiful cycle of white light extending back and forth between you and your lover.

MediDating

In addition, I have included a MediDating meditation that I've created to help demystify the dating process. For all of you who are not currently in a romantic relationship but are dating, this meditation is great before a date. It will totally hook you up and turn your light switch on before you walk out of the house. MediDate for the next thirty days.

Evening MediDation

Begin with an evening MediDation before you go to sleep. Envision your new story. See yourself on a date with this person you totally dig. Most importantly, let the vision guide you into a positive feeling. Sit in this MediDation for a minimum of five minutes.

Walking MediDation

Take your new story for a walk. As you walk to work, to the gym or out at night, hold the vision of your desired date. Let your mind bring you to the place where you feel the feeling of being with this awesome person, and enjoy the sensation. Walk around the streets vibrating this powerful feeling, and you will surely begin attracting.

The Big Night MediDation

Once you attract a great date, make sure you have fun with it. To get yourself into a full-blown positive vibration for your date, use the following Big Night MediDation as your guide. Sit in stillness for a minimum of five minutes. Envision exactly how you want the night to go, from the cab to the good night kiss. Breathe in the mantra, *"I am relaxed,"* and breathe out, *"I receive."* Take this mantra with you on the date and recite it all night long.

~ing write

~Ing write yourself a sacred contract committing to your new ways of being in a romantic relationship. Release your old behavior and consign a new vision for love. A sample contract looks like this:

> I, Michelle, am willing to change my patterns in romantic relationships. I commit to seeing my partner as equal to everything and everyone else I love in my life. I promise not to make an idol of him, and to honor him for his inner greatness rather than his frame. I forgive myself and him for my ego's illusions. From this day forward, I commit to transforming my romantic illusions into holy love.
>
> Signed,
> Michelle

Reread this contract before you go to sleep for thirty days straight. Allow it to be a gentle reminder of your dedication to the holy relationship and your release of "special love."

The upcoming chapter aims to further enhance your peace through the Climbing Equation. Take a deep breath and get ready to climb!

CHAPTER SIX

Climbing: ~ing Your Way to Higher Thoughts

Seek not to change the world, but choose to change your mind about the world.

—A Course in Miracles

Lauren's alarm clock goes off at 7 o'clock in the morning. She hits snooze for ten more minutes. The snooze is unsuccessful, as her mind has already begun its own rat race. Within seconds of opening her eyes to a new day, her ego starts telling her she sucks. Her ego says she's fat and lazy for not getting up at 6 o'clock to go to the gym. Then, still in bed, she reaches over to check her Blackberry, only to find that the guy she likes didn't text her back. To avoid feeling the pain of rejection she quickly scrolls through her e-mails. A pang of fear rushes through her as she sees an e-mail from her boss that came in at 11 o'clock last night. The e-mail includes a list of orders and expectations for the week in a threatening tone that is crystal clear even through cyberspace.

In an attempt to avoid this feeling of fear, she tries to close her eyes for ten more minutes. This never works. Her mind is racing. Her ego's thoughts immediately flood in with, "This guy will never call me back. I'm not skinny enough for him. I suck because I couldn't even get my lazy ass to the gym. Ugh, I've gained ten pounds. What the hell can I wear today? None of my pants even fit! Argh, the alarm again! Shit, it's 7:15! I have to get my ass in gear. I cannot be late again or I'm gonna get fired." Ready to admit defeat and face the literal rat race, Lauren lurches out of bed and stumbles to the bathroom, only to find that her roommate is taking her sweet ass time in the shower. Thoughts of rage overcome Lauren as she "politely" asks her roommate how long she'll be. Lauren's tone may sound sweet, but the energy and thoughts behind her request are far from kind. Her roommate replies, "I'll be a little while. I just got in, and I still have to shave my legs." Lauren feels like she is about to explode.

To change her mood, she turns on the news. Bad idea. As she gets dressed, all she can hear are the muffled voices of news anchors talking about the recession, the bailout and the numbers of unemployed people in the nation. The newscasters spin Lauren into an ego tornado of fear based on her current job circumstances. She begins to obsess over how much work she has to do and the fact that she is holding on to her job for dear life. Her fearful thoughts spin her into rush mode. She realizes that there is no time to waste because her boss will lose it if she's late again. "Screw the shower," she thinks as she puts on extra deodorant. In her rush to get ready, she rips her panty hose.

Unable to find a clean pair, she reaches into the dirty laundry and throws on yesterday's stockings. "Life sucks," she says under her breath. Charging out the door, she runs past the bagel shop, strategically avoiding breakfast. Instead she grabs a venti coffee from Starbucks and continues her sprint to work. By the time she reaches her office, she is shaking from all that coffee on an empty stomach.

With five minutes to spare, she reaches into her handbag to calm herself down with a cigarette. As she sucks in the nicotine, her mind begins racing again. She replays her to-do list four or five times, only to sabotage those thoughts with her ego's reminder that the guy never texted her back.

As the day progresses, things don't get much better. In fact they get worse. As soon as she walks into her office, her boss starts barking orders at her. The negative sound of her boss's tone makes Lauren even more fearful of losing her job. As a result, she feels stressed and anxious all day. These fearful thoughts and feelings lead her to make some serious mistakes, the worst of which is to send her boss a Gchat message that was intended for a friend. The message was, of course, a nasty comment about her boss. After she reads Lauren's message, her boss goes into a rage, makes a huge scene in front of the entire office, and fires Lauren on the spot.

This series of events—luckily—led Lauren to hit her personal rock bottom, which was actually a long time coming. Sometimes we can't make necessary changes until our outside world catches up with our internal chaos. This was the case for Lauren. She had to lose her job in order to properly take action toward cleaning up all her harmful thought patterns. She ended up in my coaching chair. In her first session I asked her gently, "What's been going on with you?" Tears welled up as she replied, "I have no idea. I feel shitty day after day. I've gained tons of weight. I lost my job. No boys like me. My mom is breathing down my neck to meet a guy. My dad is pressuring me to get a new job. And I can't see anything getting better. I'm a complete mess!" My response was, "Congratulations my friend, you've made it to the right place." In classic ~*ing* girl fashion I cheered, "You've hit your rock bottom, which means you've stopped falling. It's only up from here!"

In Lauren's case, her chaotic life situations were a mirror for the chaos in her mind. "I am affected only by my thoughts," says *A Course in Miracles*. Because Lauren's mind had gotten caught up in the ego's tornado, her energy had gotten sucked into it too. Her negative thoughts transformed into negative energy, which resulted in unfortunate circumstances. Unbeknownst to Lauren, she had created these circumstances as a result of her thoughts.

The solution was to take the steps necessary to conquer her thoughts so that she could view the world from an entirely different perspective. Furthermore, it was time for Lauren to change her ways. If she chose to stay in the mind-set of "I'm stuck and I cannot get out," then she'd remain stuck with no way out. I prepared her for climb*ing* toward a new way of thinking, the same way I'll prepare you if you're ready to overcome your negative thought patterns and change your life.

The focus of this chapter is to show the importance of conquering your negative thought patterns and learning to view life from an elevated, more positive perspective. I'll explain why climbing is a perfect ~*ing* activity for figuring out exactly how to reach that higher plane of positive thinking. Plus, you'll learn to climb out of your ego and reach for the thoughts of your highest self. In addition, you'll get a bird's-eye view of what a life filled with positive thoughts can be like. Lastly, I'll ask you to follow me as I guide you through the Mov*ing* Equation to new heights of thinking.

HOW THOUGHTS AFFECT ENERGY

Your thoughts create energy. I'm going to throw a concept out that may be new to you, but it perfectly illustrates this point. That concept is applied kinesiology, also known as "muscle testing," which was pioneered by Dr. George Goodheart. Wayne Dyer, an internationally known author and speaker in the field of self-development (and an ~*ing* Girl fave!), does a great job of explaining the concept when he says that "behind every thought is energy." According to applied kinesiology, when you think higher thoughts, such as love, kindness and joy, your energy is stronger. Alternatively, when your thoughts are focused on lower-level emotions, such as sadness, fear or anger, your energy is weakened.

To visually prove this concept during my lectures, I'll often invite a brave stranger from the audience to act as my human visual aid. I ask her to hold her arm out horizontally and resist as I press down on it. Before I press down, I ask her to think of something positive and loving. Then, when I press her arm down, she has a strong resistance to my pressure and her arm is unmovable. Next, I ask her to think of something that makes her fearful or upset. This time, when I apply pressure, her arm goes weak and drops to her side. This exercise is a powerful way of physically portraying how your thoughts inform your energy. There is no comparison between the strength of my volunteer's arm when she thinks happy thoughts and when she thinks negatively. Within seconds of changing her mind, her energy shifts from strong and powerful to weak and limp.

Furthermore, your thoughts do not only affect your own energy. All thoughts transmute energy outward. Negative thoughts are toxic and send nasty vibrations into the Universe. These vibrations are picked up by everyone around you. This is the concept of the Universal Law of Attraction, which teaches that *like attracts like*. The theory is that your lower-level vibration is attracted to other lower-level vibrations. (A lower-level vibration is akin to a negative thought.) The same goes for positive vibrations. Your positive thoughts produce stronger energy that in turn attracts more positive experiences.

Many people are unaware of their attracting power and therefore have spent a lifetime being naive about how their negative thoughts affect them. Think about it. I'm sure you know people who are always worrying. These types of people are constantly attracting more things to worry about as a result of their worried state. A day filled with worry may lead them to trip on the sidewalk and break their leg. This shows that their obsessive worrying whipped their energy into a frenzy, at which point they were moving so fast that they fell. Worry is a prayer for chaos. When your mind is stuck in a pattern of chaos, that is all you will experience. The difference between the strength of higher-level thoughts and the weakness of lower-level thoughts is dramatic. In Lauren's case, it was the difference between leaving work with a job and leaving work jobless.

CONQUERING A MOUNTAIN OF NEGATIVE THINKING

It's no fun going through life ruled by negative thoughts that in turn create negative experiences. For that reason I've designed the Climb*ing* Equation, which will guide you to consciously choose powerfully charged, happy thoughts that will result in awesome outcomes. The ego is often born out of feelings of low self-worth; when you climb, you start off at a low point and are working to pull yourself upward.

In the Climb*ing* Equation, what you're climbing toward is the thoughts of your higher self, which are fueled by the voice of your *inner guide*. Climbing out of your negative thought patterns requires strength and commitment. With the will to change and the courage to climb, you can defy the ego's gravitational pull and reach your higher self. The goal is to choose to pull your thoughts to an altitude that is higher than your ego. Each day your ego is waiting to attempt to pull you down to its level. Therefore, embrace the attitude of *progress, not perfection,* and if you find yourself falling down a notch or two, don't fret—just dust yourself off, lift yourself up and keep on climbing.

A VIEW FROM THE TOP

The goal of climbing your way to your higher self is to permanently change your beliefs. When you believe that your life is hooked up, everything *is* hooked up!

Prepare for hip results when you start choosing to change your mind. When your thoughts align with love, they ignite your good vibrations. When your vibrations are aligned with good stuff, you are 100 percent attracting good stuff. For example, when Lauren began practicing the Climb*ing* Equation, her chaotic thought patterns began to wane. As a result of her dedication to the Climb*ing* Equation, her mind calmed down. Her new relaxed thoughts led her to have more chilled-out energy. She enjoyed this new way of being, and everyone else did too. People noticed her changes immediately. By reaching new heights with her thoughts and energy, Lauren was able to secure a new job. And, best of all, instead of becoming mired down in the inevitable challenges of life, she learned to embrace them as opportunities for growth.

CLIMB*ing* YOUR WAY TO NEW THOUGHTS

The ~*ing* Equation will begin as usual with rethink*ing*. I'll guide you through tools that will help you climb your way out of negative thought patterns toward more powerful beliefs. Next you will add the activity of rock-climbing to show your body what it feels like to reach the heights of happiness. (As usual, there will be additional activities suggested. There are a slew of activities that mimic the same physical challenges and mental exertion as climbing. As with climbing, these activities also allow you to physically lift yourself up.) Then I'll guide you into a meditation which will help further the mental reconditioning by overcoming your negative thoughts and transforming them into higher thoughts of self-love. To receive guidance for moving forward, you will ~*ing write* an entirely new belief system based on the higher, more positive mindset you will be aspiring to.

Before you embark on your climb, take a moment to assess your thought patterns. In order to do that, ask yourself the following questions: *Do you feel stuck in obsessive thought patterns? For instance, are you constantly checking your crush's Facebook page? Or are you obsessing about what you ate last night? Do you constantly compare yourself to other people? Do your negative thoughts breed more negativity in your life? Do you over-think everything?*

THE CLIMB*ing* EQUATION—
Thirty Days to Higher Thoughts

STEP ONE: Rethink*ing*

Why waste any more time thinking negatively? Let's clean up the crazy and clear space for your ~*ing*. Changing your mind is the crux of the ~*ing* work, and it cannot be taken lightly. In this case, it's all about climbing above the thoughts that bring you to a low place and replacing them with thoughts that lift you to new heights. Let's begin the rethinking climb with a method I call the Three Rs— Recognize, Record, Release.

To Recognize, put a rubber band around your wrist. The rubber band is a tool you'll use as a gentle reminder to shift your thinking. Whenever your ego acts out, you will snap the band against your arm. Snap your rubber band each time you Recognize any negative thoughts or uncomfortable feelings. Next up is Record. To record, put your pen to paper and write *"I block myself when I listen to my ego say* _____."

Fill in the blank with whatever ego delusion is blocking you from happiness in that moment. In Lauren's case, her Record step looked like this: "I block myself when I listen to my ego say I'm too fat." Or "I block myself when I listen to my ego say I cannot get a new job."

Finally, rock out the third R: Release. Take a deep breath and feel the feeling that comes over you when your ego starts in with a nasty delusion. For ninety seconds, allow yourself to just *be* with the feelings that come up. Remember that all of your overthinking is just you *thinking over* unhealed feelings. Let the feeling pass through you, and honor it for what it is. On the exhale, release it to the Universe. In your mind, say, *I choose love and I release fear. I welcome a shift in perception.*

The more you repeat the process of the Three Rs, the easier it will be to identify the power of your ego. In his book *The Power of Now*, Eckhart Tolle refers to the process of recognizing the ego as becoming the "witness to the thinker." When you witness the ego, you stop it in its tracks. By recording its illusion, you disassociate with the ego's nightmare. You *"witness the thinker."* In the Release step, you shine light on the darkness and relinquish its control. This exercise will guide you to disassociate with the ego and even begin to see yourself differently. It takes necessary, diligent action to pull yourself out of the darkness, but it's way worth it when you do. "The fundamental change will occur with the change of mind in the thinker," says *A Course in Miracles.*

An additional tool you can apply to the rethinking step is what I like to call the "positive thought ladder." Basically, whenever a negative thought crosses your mind, simply climb up the ladder using the positive thoughts of your ~*ing* as your guide. You can begin your climb the moment you identify a feeling of negative emotion. The technique is quite simple. You literally climb from fear-based thoughts on up to higher thoughts by talking yourself into a new positive thought process. For example: Anna finds herself feeling uncomfortable, and she recognizes her thoughts saying, *"You ate too much today and you look fat."* Instead of falling down the fear hole and eating poorly for the rest of the day, Anna decides to climb. She actively reaches for better thoughts, which go like this: *"It's fine that I ate what I wanted because I worked out last night, and I feel great about that. I can go to the gym later today, and I can enjoy a healthy salad for dinner. I don't have to get upset every time I eat something that isn't on my diet. I recognize that these thoughts are my ego and instead I choose to believe that I'm healthy and beautiful."*

Use the Three Rs and the positive thought ladder on a daily basis for the next thirty days. I still need to do both of these exercises every day of my life in order to stay aligned with my ~ing. Your negative thoughts are sure to come back more often than not. But know you have two powerful tools in your back pocket that will help you climb your way out of the ego's illusion at any given moment.

STEP TWO: Rethinking + Moving

Moving with your rethinking tools will enhance your mental climb. One of the best activities to apply to the Climbing Equation is rock climbing, which these days can be done on a rock wall at your local gym. My buddy Ivan Greene is a rock-climbing legend. He started climbing back in the late '80s and co-wrote the definitive bouldering guide: *Bouldering in the Shawangunks.* Ivan says, "Climbing is the greatest way to get out of your head. Allowing thoughts to serve, not lead. The joy of being while climbing. That is the essence of this art. The ability to go beyond limiting thoughts and preconceived ideas of what is possible, like *I am too short, I am too weak, I am too heavy, too big, I've never done this before, that wall is so high*. Climb*ing* helps you say 'shhhhhh' to all those negative thoughts."

Once I went climbing with Ivan at the Chelsea Piers rock wall in New York City. Following his lead, I hit the wall with the intention of clearing my mind and reaching my own new heights. At the beginning of the climb, my thoughts were filled with fear. Not only was I afraid of the heights I was about to scale, but I was also holding on to some residual ego fear from earlier in the day. My ego had gotten me all tripped up over a fight I'd had with a friend. I was fearful that we wouldn't make up and that our resentment toward each other would never go away. As I began to climb, I made the commitment to reach for better thoughts with each move upward. With each new physical height, I chose a new and better thought about my friend. As I moved farther and farther up the wall, I envisioned myself moving further away from my ego. By the time I reached the top, I felt exhilarated by the climb and had completely changed my mind about my friend. As soon as I hit the ground I called her to apologize.

An additional activity that will physically help your ~*ing* guide you above the ego is hik*ing*. I've taken my ego on a hike many a time. At the bottom of the hill or mountain, I'll set my intention to reach for higher thoughts. As I hike up, I'll climb my thoughts into higher levels with each step I take. Physically and mentally I'll climb my way to a better vibration and into my higher self. By the time I reach the top of the mountain, I'm feeling great. I feel an overarching sense of release. I've successfully climbed my way into a new way of thinking and can enjoy the view from the top. (Other activities you can apply include the stairmaster or even walking on the treadmill at an incline.)

STEP THREE: Receiving (Meditating/~*ing write*)

Meditation is the most significant tool for climbing out of the ego and receiving the higher thoughts of your *inner guide*. To enhance your climb*ing* mediation, I suggest adding music. Simply turn on one of your favorite upbeat songs and sit in a meditation with the music playing. Allow the music to guide you out of the ego and back to joy. To take this one step further, you can create a "positive perception" playlist, a compilation of songs that make you feel great. My positive perception playlist has songs like Stevie Wonder's "Superstition," White Snake's "Here I Go Again" and Sarah McLaughlin's "Ordinary Miracles." Dig into your music collection and create a positive perception playlist. When you recognize your ego's got you in a headlock, you can immediately turn this on and embark on a music meditation.

For further climbing let me guide you on a meditative climb from ego to the *inner guidance* of your higher self. (Download my audio meditation at www.addmoreing.com.)

Close your eyes, take a deep breath in and exhale slowly.

Envision yourself at the bottom of a mountain.

As you look up, you see a beautiful light shining from the top of the mountain.

You choose to climb toward this light.

This light represents higher levels of thinking.

With each step, you climb closer and closer to the light of your higher thoughts.

Breathe in—I choose to reach for better thoughts.

Breathe out—I will climb away from the darkness and to the heights of the light.

Breathe in—I have courage to climb.

With each new height, you feel lighter and lighter as you move further away from your ego's illusions.

Breathe out—I climb higher and reach for higher thoughts.

Breathe in—I'm guided toward the light.

Breathe out—I release my ego as I reach higher.

Breath in—I welcome the top of the mountain and let go of low-level thinking.

As you reach the top, feel a sense of release come over you.

I choose to change my vision.

I choose love over fear.

My mind is clear and I accept miracles.

See yourself as you look over the edge of the mountain, looking down on your old view, reveling in the view of the higher-level world.

~ing write

Following every climb*ing* activity, I suggest you flow right into a climb*ing write*. Maximize your time in the ~*ing zone* and bring your higher-level ideas to the page. By writing your new thoughts down after a climb*ing* activity, you imprint your subconscious with new ways of thinking.

To further maximize these shifted thoughts, use your climb*ing write* all day long. My suggestion is to bring a small notebook with you everywhere for the next thirty days. This notebook will be used for practicing your Three Rs and to facilitate your stream-of-conscious climb*ing writes*.

If you're ready to climb to even greater heights, I suggest thirty days of morn*ing write*. Morning is the best time to strap on your mind's billet belt and begin climbing. Julia Cameron, the world-renowned transformational author of *The Artist's Way*, created a very famous exercise called "morning pages." I've included the *~ing* girl version in this section to provide you with a transformational tool. The morning is when your mind is the most impressionable and therefore the optimal time for the ego to bring you down. Instead of starting your day with chaotic thoughts, begin climb*ing* as soon as your alarm goes off. Climb with an *~ing write*. Keep a notebook next to your bed and *~ing write* for ten minutes. Let your ego dump onto the page and release any negative ideas. When you feel a sense of release, start reaching for higher and higher thoughts as you *~ing write* your way to an elevated plane.

Every day is a new chance to climb your way to a better life. Don't worry about yesterday or what will happen tomorrow. Just focus on the climb in front of you and make your way to the top.

I hope you've begun to experience some powerful changes throughout your *~ing* journey. Guess what, my friend? You've only just begun! Get planted on your yoga mat, because the next Equation will have you stretch*ing* even further.

CHAPTER SEVEN

Stretching: Beyond the Ego's Backlash

You who are beginning to wake are still aware of dreams and have not yet forgotten them.

—A Course in Miracles

Our deepest fear is not that we are inadequate. Our deepest fear is that we are powerful beyond all measure. It is our light, not our darkness, that frightens us the most. We ask ourselves, Who am I to be brilliant, gorgeous, talented, famous? Actually, who are you not to be? You are a child of God. Your playing small doesn't serve the world.

A Return to Love *by Marianne Williamson*

Mary sat quietly in the group coaching circle. It was obvious that something was bothering her. Her energy was low and she seemed out of sorts. I went around the room and checked in with each person, confident that when I got to Mary she'd open up. For four months I'd been coaching this group and they'd experienced a lot of miracles. Mary, in particular, had truly committed to the work. Like a perfect ~*ing* student, she asked all the right questions, did all her ~*ing* homework and followed through with making real changes in her life. Then, predictably, her ego punctured her pink cloud. Finally, when the roundtable check-in reached Mary, I asked her what was up. She replied, "I'm not sure, Gab. I've been doing the ~*ing* work like a full-time job. I'd gotten to a place where I felt amazing, but out of nowhere my ego started to take me down. Now I feel stuck again." I told Mary to take a deep breath. I explained that this was totally natural and I'd witnessed situations like this countless times.

What Mary was dealing with is what I call "ego backlash." Ego backlash is kind of like falling off the wagon while on the ~ing journey. The darkness of Mary's ego couldn't survive in the light of her ~ing. Her dedication to her ~ing freed Mary of her ego's resentment toward others and toward herself. As it says in the Course, "The ego cannot survive without judgment." This was the good news. The bad news was that as soon as her ego got wind of Mary's ~ing campaign, it revved up for its comeback. The Course teaches that the ego is "Suspicious at best and vicious at worst." Ego will drag you down right when it senses your thoughts climbing up. The ego will actually do pushups while you sleep.

Not surprisingly, Mary wasn't alone in facing her ego's backlash. After she shared her struggle, others spoke up about theirs. Kelly shared that she'd been dedicated to her ~ing until she got into a relationship. After that, her ego took serious advantage of her romantic illusions by bringing up all of her old fears. Then Alisa spoke up. She'd totally committed to her ~ing, even proclaiming out loud to her friends that she was no longer going to "play small." However, the week after her announcement, her ego burst in with fear talk. All of Alisa's old anxieties rushed back in. Thoughts like, "How can I play big in life when I still have tons of financial insecurity and fear of people? I am a fraud." After Alisa spoke up, several others at the roundtable began complaining of their own ego backlash instances. I calmed the group down by informing them that this was totally normal.

I went on to explain that I too had experienced an ego backlash early on in my own ~ing practice. Indeed, when I first embraced my ~ing I was willing to do whatever it took to feel better. Like Mary, I was the perfect ~ing student, and ~inged my way to a powerful pink cloud. But after three months things started to shift.

My negative thoughts began to creep back in. Old emotional patterns reared their nasty heads. When the ego started to slink back, I felt as though all my hard work had been for nothing. The ego's fear began roaring in my ear and it was hard to ignore.

I was so distraught when this happened that I had to reach out for help. So I called a mentor of mine named Erica. She laughed when I told her what had happened. She said, "I expected this call. Many times when things start to get good, we tend to stop working as hard. That allows the ego to slip back in. So the best thing to do when things get good is to actually work harder. Remember, it works if you work it." In addition, Erica taught me that whenever I'd slack on my ~*ing* work, life would be more difficult to navigate. Boy, was she right! Anytime I'd get a new boyfriend and lose track of my ~*ing*, I'd end up making him my idol, and as a result the relationship would collapse. After this happened, I tended to run right back to my ~*ing* work. This went for anything I put before my ~*ing*. Whenever I stopped exercising my daily ~*ing* routine, I'd immediately feel the ego sneak back in. "Sneak" is the operative word. The sneaky ego will always find tricky ways to deny the light of your ~*ing*.

In this chapter, I'm going to give you a heads-up on some of the ego's sneakiest tricks for worming its way back in. Then I'm going to explain how you can overcome this by revving up your ~*ing* practice. I'll also share the perfect ~*ing* activity for getting beyond the ego's backlash—stretch*ing*. Lastly, I'll walk you through the Stretch*ing* Equation, which is guaranteed to shine light on the ego's bag of tricks and bring your thoughts back to love.

THE SNEAKY EGO'S BAG OF TRICKS

Your ego has been hanging out with you for so many years that eventually it's the only voice you hear. The ego stuffs you into a box where you only feel safe living in fear and playing small. Therefore, whenever you step outside the box and shine light on the darkness, the ego freaks out and amps up its game. By this point in the book you've called on the light of your ~*ing*, and as expected, your ego will do everything in its power to extinguish its light. Remember, the darkness of the ego cannot survive in the light of your *inner guide*. So as the light slowly begins to brighten, the ego freaks and begins pulling out all the stops to put it out. Below is the ~*ing* girl interpretation of how the *Course* describes the ego's comeback.

Trick One: Dredging Up That Old Fear Talk

One of the ego's favorite responses to the light is tons of fear talk. When your ~*ing* work gets strong, the ego will dredge up any old fear from your past to turn down the light. Ego will clutch on to fears of people, money, romance, self image, being alone, you name it. It will taunt you with warnings like, "This happiness cannot possibly last." "This relationship is too good to be true." "You'd better get a job and let go of those entrepreneurial visions." "Get back together with that guy who hurt you because you might not find someone else."

Trick Two: Guilt

Choosing to identify with the ego's backlash always results in feelings of guilt. You experience this guilt because you've turned your back on your ~*ing* and chosen the ego's fearful attack. Whether you know it or not, you feel as though you've committed a crime against your ~ing by turning your back on it. Then, unconsciously, these negative thoughts are reflected in nasty feelings and beliefs about yourself. There is an overarching sense of unworthiness, the guilty, unworthy feeling then leads you into self-sabotage mode. The ego will convince you that because you've denied your ~ing for a hot second, you've lost touch with the light entirely, the journey is over, and now you have no choice but to surrender once again to the ego's darkness. Your negative thoughts will escalate, bringing you back down.

For instance, Jennifer's ego told her to eat a full pie of pizza just because she fell off her diet for a few days! Her ego said, "Well, you failed. Your diet's over, might as well go for the gusto!" Her guilt over slipping on her diet spun her into self-sabotage. To clarify this further, her guilt was not actually about her diet. Instead, she unconsciously felt guilty about denying the peaceful voice of her ~ing. Her ego grabbed on to the slightest missed step and amplified it further, which took her further away from her ~ing. The further she got from her ~ing, the more guilt she felt because she had separated from her *inner guide*.

Trick Three: Denial

Left with the anxiety and guilt over turning your back on your ~ing, your only recourse is to return to the ego for help. The ego makes you think you can be "saved" from this guilt by simply denying it. In order for the ego to survive, it has to convince you that your ~ing isn't real and that you must deny feeling guilty over leaving it behind. (Remember, you feel guilty because you've chosen your ego over your ~ing.) If you address this guilt, you'll go back to your ~ing. Therefore, the ego will start to rationalize your guilt. In Jennifer's case her ego rationalized not sticking to her diet and then sucked her back into her old habits of overeating. I've often heard John Assaraf, author of the best-selling book *Having It All*, break the word "rationalize" into two words to get "rational lies." He's got that one right! The ego is telling you a bunch of rational lies to keep you from staying close to the light.

Trick Four: Attack

Finally, after the ego's convinced you to deny the guilt of separating from your ~*ing*, it will take its tricks one step farther. The ego takes your guilt and projects it onto others. This is a cheap trick because instead of looking inward for a sense of relief, the ego turns your guilt toward other people. This is what the *Course* refers to as "magic." The ego thinks that if we project our guilt onto others, we'll "magically" be free of it by unconsciously placing it outside ourselves. This is when we go into attack mode. The ego will begin attacking others in an effort to sabotage your happiness. The ego disguises these attacks as protection. These attacks are merely projections of your own fears placed on the world in an effort to keep you in the darkness. In Jennifer's case, her guilty feelings from overeating a pizza led her ego to deny the guilt by projecting onto her friend who eats super healthy. Her ego said, "She's a crazy vegan who never has any fun. I'm not inviting her to dinner tonight."

In addition, the ego will attack *you*. The ego's perception of you is that you're unloving and unforgiving. Therefore, when you bring any kind of loving thoughts into your life, your ego will become "suspicious and vicious" and attack. This attack will play out with thoughts like, "You can't love your mother, she totally ruined your life." You will be made to feel wrong for choosing love because that is not the perception of the ego. The ego will attack anything and anyone in its effort to avoid the light.

TRICKSTER RECAP

To pull this all together, I'll break it down one more time, ~ing girl style. Your work in the past six chapters has shined light on the ego's darkness. By choosing to think with your ~ing over your ego, life began to get better. Then, predictably, the ego freaked out because it knows it cannot survive in the light of your ~ing. At which point the ego revved up with nasty fear talk. The fear talk made you feel funky and possibly led you to act out in some way directed by the ego. Then you started to feel even funkier because you knew you'd pushed your ~ing away in favor of your ego. At this point the ego knows that the guilt you feel about turning your back on your ~ing will guide you back to the light. Therefore the ego makes you deny this feeling of separation from your ~ing by "magically" projecting your negative feelings onto others. Then you go into attack mode by placing all of your fears onto others rather than letting your ~ing clean them up. The ego makes you attack others with your own fears so that it can keep you stuck in the box of living fearful and small. The attack keeps the fear story going rather than allowing your ~ing to step in for cleanup. By this point you're sucked back into the dark hole of the ego and have turned off the flashlight your *inner guide* would have used to lead you out.

REVVING UP YOUR ~*ing* PRACTICE

Now that you're on to the ego's tricks, you have a better understanding of why it's important to rev up your ~*ing* practice. This
requires stretch*ing* beyond the ego's fear and welcoming in *even more*
light. I understand that your life is busy with friends, work, etc. But
remember, the ego cannot survive in the light, and life will flow
with ease when you maintain a daily commitment to your ~*ing*.

Even the ~*ing* girl never stops ~*inging*. Just because I've got
my ~*ing* down to a science doesn't mean I've finished my work. If I
stopped connecting to my ~*ing* today, I guarantee I'd feel super
guilty and things would get pretty funky, fast. The days where I've
put my work, relationships, money, whatever, before my ~*ing* are
days that life stops flowing. Because I've taken myself through all
of the ~*ing* Equations, I now use them interchangeably. Sometimes
I'll mix up the Equation daily and other times I'll revisit a full-blown
thirty-day journey to transform a specific area of my life.

For instance, last month I spent thirty days in the Feel*ing*
Equation. I'd uncovered some new stuff I hadn't addressed yet, so
I chose to feel for thirty and continue my journey of release. Other
times I may spend a full thirty days in the Forgiv*ing* Equation if
there is a person or situation that needs to be released. In most
cases I flow with my ~*ing* Equation daily depending on what I've
got going on. In order to maintain my ~*ing*, my typical day looks
like this: I start my day with a twenty-minute meditation followed
by an hour of physical activity (running, dancing, rollerblading,
rebounding, you name it). I'm at my desk by 8 AM. Throughout the
day, I exercise the "F" word by forgiving everyone I see. I forgive
the lady who knocks into me on the street, I forgive the bank teller
who won't smile, I forgive my friend for not calling me back. Most

importantly, I forgive myself all day long for any behavior that is not ~*ing* worthy.

In addition, I spot-check my thoughts on a moment-by-moment basis. If a funky feeling comes up, I sit for ninety seconds and check in with my ~*ing* to explore what's going on inside. I get curious about the feeling and don't try to push it away. When I feel a sense of relief, I then start climb*ing*. I use the Three Rs to climb my way out of nasty thoughts, or I sit in another meditation. Finally, at night, I cozy up with a book. This is when I say a bunch of prayers and thank the Universe for hookin' me up yet another day. I ~*ing write* for twenty and then hit the pillow for some Zs. Often, I'm woken up between 3 and 4 AM. At this time, I take advantage of my cleared thoughts and I sit up in bed in a meditation. There is something magical that happens to me at these times. Beautiful thoughts flood through me as I sit. Then I ~*ing write* for a bit. Many powerful new ideas come to me in the wee hours of the morning.

S-T-R-E-T-C-H-*ing*!

I don't expect everyone to jump right in and be as dedicated to their ~*ing* work as I am. But I do suggest taking this time to stretch your work a little further. That's why I've created the Stretch*ing* Equation to help you out. This Equation will require that you commit mentally and physically to Stretch*ing* even further. I've chosen to call this the Stretch*ing* Equation because when you stretch you take your muscles beyond where they are at rest. When you perform a stretch, you actually have a physical feeling of "Oh, it hurts so good!" Afterward, the part of your body that you stretched feels reinvigorated and tingly because of the blood flow and oxygen it has received from the stretch. Just like when you stretch a muscle, when you take your ~ing practice a little further than where you've gotten comfortable with it, you stretch your mind past the pain and discomfort and introduce a new understanding of relief. Each time you stretch past your ego you create a new pattern in your brain that says ~ing is good and ego is no good. The more often you stretch in the direction of your ~ing, the further you get from associating yourself with your ego.

THE STRETCH

Before you begin the Stretching Equation I'll guide you to spot-checking where the ego's been playing nasty tricks. This will help you take a closer look at how the ego has resisted your light. Then you'll begin with a series of rethinking exercises to help you convert the ego's tricks into miracles. Then, further supporting the Equation, I've used the moving section to highlight anecdotes and interviews with some of the hippest yogis in the country. They will each share personal experiences of how their stretching practice has guided them past the ego's illusion and into the light. Next is the receiving section where your mental stretch will settle in. Your meditation will be a time to make a further commitment to the light. I've included a new mantra to enhance your dedication to choosing love over fear and light over darkness. You'll finish up receiving with your ~ing write. This will be the time to receive a truthful inventory of how dedicated you've been to your ~*ing* and how willing you've been to stretch past the ego's backlash.

I challenge you to stretch beyond your limiting beliefs and surrender to the ~*ing* process for another round of thirty days. If you've been workin your ~*ing*, I assume you've experienced many miraculous moments of light along the way. But now it's time to take more steps over the bridge from your old life to a new life led by ~*ing*. Trust that your ~*ing* will light your path. Stretch and be guided.

Before you begin the Stretch*ing* Equation, start by spot-check*ing* where the ego's been playing nasty tricks. The goal of this step will be to take a closer look at how the ego has resisted your light. *Has your pink cloud burst? Do you feel your ego trying to creep back in? Have you noticed your positive thoughts shift back to old ideas? Have you begun to attack people you have already forgiven? Do you feel guilty?*

THE STRETCH*ing* EQUATION
—Thirty Days to Stretch Beyond the Ego's Backlash

STEP ONE: Rethink*ing*
Begin by making a list of the situations where your ego gets the best of you, possibly in romantic relationships, in your job, when you spend time with family, etc. Be specific. What new nasty stories is your ego telling you? Get clear about where the ego's been triggering your fears.

Turning On Your Light Switch

Karen Salmansohn suggested that I use the light switches in my home as reminders to turn on my inner light. I loved this idea, and decorated each of my light switches with notes reminding me to turn on my *inner light*.

Decorate your light switches. Write notes on them like, *"I choose ~ing over ego."* Or *"I turn on my light."* Each time you turn on a light, ask yourself, *How have I connected with my inner guide today? Has my ego been acting up?* Use this simple action to activate your *inner light* daily.

The following exercises will help you stretch beyond your ego on a moment-by-moment basis. Keep turning on your light switch by actively practicing the following rethink*ing* steps. Use these tools as gentle reminders that you are not your ego.

Laughter

This is a tool straight from the *Course*. It suggests that we do not take the ego's illusions seriously. When we listen to the ego, we make it real in our minds. Instead, the *Course* suggests that we laugh gently at the ego's "tiny, mad idea." Use your rubber band, and each time your ego acts up, snap it as a reminder to laugh at the ego's delusional mischief. This step will guide you further in the process of stopping the ego in its tracks.

Out the Ego

In instances when the ego makes you nuts with fearful illusions about another person, it can sometimes be fun to bring the silly lies to the surface. For instance, I once made up an entire story in my head about my boyfriend cheating on me. I played this story out for several hours. I tried asking for miracles, laughing if off and meditating. Finally I stepped away from my meditation pillow, called him and outed my ego. I told him about my ridiculous story and together we laughed it off. Bring your light *out* of the darkness.

Stop Future Tripping

Future illusions are of the ego. When you start focusing on the future, you eventually get tripped up. It's super easy for the ego to find fear when the future is involved. Remember that all future projections are situations that do not exist. When you find yourself getting heady about the future, take a deep breath and say out loud, *"I'm right where I need to be."*

Smile

When your ego's got you in a headlock break out with a long EEEEEEE. It sounds super silly, but you can't help but smile when you make that sound. Smiling leads to laughing, and laughing shines light on the ego. Keep it simple with a smile.

- Ask for a miracle: As soon as you finish laughing, release your ego further by asking your *inner guide* for some help. Simply say out loud: *"I choose to see this differently. I ask the Universe to guide me toward a shift in perception."*
- Forgive again: Given the fact that the ego loves to attack others when it feels threatened, it's a good idea to stay close to your forgiveness practice. Take daily inventory of whom your ego has judged (including yourself). At night, review the list of those you have attacked and release these thoughts and actions with a forgiveness prayer. Simply say out loud: *"I choose to forgive this person as I know my attack was*

merely a projection of my ego." For further protection from the ego's attack trick, make a point to forgive others and yourself all day long.

Serving

One of the best ways to step out of the darkness and back into the light is through service. Helping others immediately gets you out of your own head and away from the ego's tricky fear spiral. By bringing love to others through service, you amplify the light inside yourself. Being of service can be as simple as picking up the phone to check in with a friend, or helping an elder cross the street. If you are a woman, you can use my Web site www.herfuture.com (the social network for women to find mentors and be mentors) anytime you want to help another woman. There are thousands of women on this site helping each other daily. The feedback I receive from them is that they *always* feel better after they've reached out to help someone through kind words, sharing a quote or simply responding on a message board. Shine light on others and reignite the light in you.

An ~ing Mantra

Retell the ego's tricky stories on a moment-by-moment basis by reciting the mantra, "I stretch beyond my ego's tricks and choose love over fear." Recite this mantra throughout the day. The next step is to stretch with it.

STEP TWO: Rethinking + Moving

Now take your new mantra and do some stretching. You may want to take this mantra with you to a yoga or pilates class, or possibly take it to the park for some light stretching. Use your body to reinforce your thoughts and stretch beyond your limiting beliefs. The power behind stretching with your affirmation is that you are making a statement to the Universe that you are willing to stretch further. Allow your affirmation to guide you toward stretching past all emotional and physical discomfort.

To further explain how the physical stretch*ing* practice can enhance your mental stretch, I've called on one of the country's hippest yogis for advice, my girl Latham Thomas, founder of Tender Shoots Wellness. Latham says, "When we stretch ourselves on the mat, finding extension, reaching through all parts of our physical being, we also stretch our consciousness and find expansion in our minds and subsequently our hearts. That's why yoga is so effective for so many people, because it stretches you to your limit physically and removes the obstacles for growth." Another power yogi is my friend Rolf Gates. Rolf suggests practicing yoga to stretch forward in all areas of your life. Rolf says, "The opposite of a retreat into fear is stepping forward with faith."

STEP THREE: Receiv*ing* (Meditat*ing*/~*ing write*)
Do the stretch*ing* meditation immediately following some kind of physical stretch. For ten minutes, stretch your mind with the affirmation, *I stretch beyond my ego, I choose love over fear, I choose love.* And breathe out, *I release my fear.*

~*ing write*
Immediately following your meditation, begin your ~*ing write.* Stretch yourself by elongating your ~*ing write* for an additional five minutes. Just write whatever you are feeling at that particular moment. Write for as long as possible, allowing any ego-driven thoughts to become transformed into love.

I hope you feel a sense of relief now knowing that you can always redirect an ego backlash right back to your ~*ing*. Each moment is a clean slate and an opportunity to release fear and stretch toward love. Remember, "It works if you work it!"

Now that you've got some serious ~*ing* tools under your belt, it's time to start playing big. Step into a phone booth, strap on a cape and prepare for some quantum shift*ing*.

CHAPTER EIGHT

Quantum Shifting: Life's Phone Booth Moments

You will remember everything the instant you desire it wholly.

—A Course in Miracles

People always say change takes time. Indeed, the majority of change requires commitment and daily repetition, but there are cases in which major life shifts can occur overnight. These types of instant changes come to those who are truly open to them, at times that are called "quantum moments." The outcome of a quantum moment is a quantum shift, which results in allowing you to change your perception of who you are and what you can accomplish. Quantum moments are actually opportunities to reinvent yourself. Think of them as life's phone-booth moments. In a quantum moment, geeky Clark Kent did a presto-chango in the nearest phone booth, and *bam!* He became a badass flying superhero *with a cape!*

However, in these moments major stuff doesn't have to happen in the world around you because the shift occurs on the inside. For example, someone could go from perceiving themselves as being high-strung to, in an instant, deciding to live with a more laid-back attitude. And simply by making that decision, the change occurs and the individual begins to face life with a new attitude. Or someone could suffer from a nasty substance addiction, wake up one morning, choose sobriety, and from there on out, never touch another drug or drop of alcohol again. More commonly, quantum shifts are about deciding who you want to be and then going for it. I've seen many cases where people have been completely stuck in one state of mind and in a quantum moment decide to completely change their perception of who they are. From there a complete shift takes place. Just by making that quantum shift in their own perception of who they are, they begin to take the steps necessary to actually become that person. Because it really is true that if you believe in yourself you will have the confidence to do what it takes to be who you want to be. The quantum shift requires an open mind and a deep desire to release the chains of the past. By surrendering your past and accepting a new perception of your present—and most importantly, a new perception of yourself— you'll realize that change is available in an instant (the cape is optional).

Right about now you're probably wondering what you need to do to make a quantum moment happen. As usual, my friends, the answer is ~ing! That's right. There is an ~ing Equation designed to help you capture your own quantum moment. But before I guide you through this special ~ing Equation, I will first give you a better sense of why quantum moments are so empowering. Then we'll take a look at some folks who have benefited from their own quantum shifts. Finally, I will walk you through the Quantum Shifting Equation which will help you seize the quantum moments in your life to become the person you want to be.

SUPERYOU!

I've experienced several quantum moments in my life. The first occurred three months after I graduated from college. I left school with a BFA in theatre and no desire to be an actress. I was paralyzed with fear about my future. My ego tormented me with thoughts like: "You're not smart enough to get a job. Your theatre degree won't get you anywhere." These thoughts continued for several months after graduation. Though I was filled with fear, I did have some fire under my ass to get working. In order to pay my bills, I hustled a few odd jobs. I promoted parties at nightclubs, executed sales and events for an energy drink company, and planned parties for a local matchmaker. I got pretty good at juggling multiple profit centers. Nonetheless, I was in an endless battle with my ego, trying to figure out how to define myself in the career world. I felt inadequate whenever anyone would ask me what I did for a living. Even though I was fully supporting myself financially I still felt *less than* everyone around me.

After three months of obsessive negative self-talk, I decided I was done feeling crappy about myself. With an open mind and a strong desire to change, I experienced my first quantum moment. I remember it like it was yesterday. Like any other morning, I woke up, immediately hopped on the Internet, and logged on to check my e-mail. There waiting for me in my inbox was an e-mail from a girl I had just met the night before. The subject line read, "You're the best hostess!" The party I'd thrown was the launch of a new nightclub in downtown Manhattan. I was super great at coordinating these types of events and making people feel really good about being there. The entire e-mail raved about how great my party had been and what a wonderful hostess I was.

The girl concluded by writing that she hoped my "company" would add her to its mailing list so she could be invited to future events. "Hmm . . . 'company,'" I thought. "I like the sound of that!" In that moment my *inner voice* said to me, "Of course you can have your own company! You are amazing at planning parties and promoting spaces. You are an entrepreneur! Start a publicity and events firm!" I knew I was onto something good. This was my first quantum moment.

From that point forward, I was never the same. I completely changed my story, internally and externally. The quantum shift was that I went from being totally insecure about my work to having a deep inner conviction that my career was hooked up and that I was a successful entrepreneur. I totally changed my perception of myself. And soon everyone around me did too. My family and friends stopped asking me when I was going to get a job. The mirror had shifted from me perceiving myself as worthless and the world reflecting that, to a more powerful reflection of my newfound confidence.

After two months I found a business partner and incorporated my first company. I was twenty-one at the time. I have been an entrepreneur ever since. All it took was the desire to change my perception of myself and the willingness to follow my *inner guidance.* Today, when I give interviews on what it takes to be a young entrepreneur a lot of people ask me, "Were you afraid to start your own business?" I always reply, "I was more afraid *not* to."

One of the great things about the possibility of a quantum moment is that it validates the idea that we really are in control of our destinies. By taking advantage of the opportunity to shift your perception of yourself that a quantum moment allows you, you are given your own superpower—the power to change the course of your life. In the blink of an eye, you can take your life in a whole different direction just by making the decision to change with all of your heart and soul. Again, not all change can be achieved so effortlessly. But this is one kind of change—the quantum shift of your perception of yourself, that hinges solely on your willingness to change— your desire to become the person you want to be.

To further inspire you to embrace the possibility of a quantum shift in your own life, I've identified five individuals who are known for overcoming adversity and turning it into greatness. This might be pure speculation on my part, but I believe these folks faced their own quantum moments when they decided to make the quantum shift that led them down their individual paths to success. I'll begin with Beethoven. Before Beethoven became known as one of the world's greatest composers, it is said that he was perceived by his teachers as hopeless. Not to mention, in the middle of his career he lost his hearing. At that point he had two choices: either give in to his adversity and quit, or continue on as a composer. Luckily, he saw past what the world thought of him and went on to compose great masterpieces.

Thomas Edison is another example. Edison is considered one of the most radical inventors in history, holding 1,093 U.S. patents. As a young boy, his teacher told him he was too stupid. He tried over 9,000 experiments before he created the first successful lightbulb. Luckily he never gave up either, or we'd be stuck in the dark!. Next is sports icon Michael Jordon. Michael is the greatest basketball player of all time. Today he's a legend, but before joining the NBA, he was just an everyday kid who was cut from the high school basketball team. Another example is legendary film director Steven Spielberg. His many groundbreaking films have made him insanely influential and outrageously successful. But he was not always a success. In fact, Spielberg dropped out of junior high school, and when he returned he was placed in a learning-disabled class. He only lasted a month in this class before he experienced a quantum shift and never looked for validation from the outside world again.

Finally, there's Albert Einstein, the most important scientist of the 20th century, who was awarded the 1921 Nobel Prize for physics. Yet, when Einstein was young, his parents thought he was mentally retarded. His teachers were so concerned about his grades that they reportedly said, "Einstein, you will never amount to anything!" Mind-blowing, right? These people who we perceive as iconic figures of success were all faced at some point with a crossroads in their lives, and I believe they experienced a quantum moment in which they decided to embrace a completely new perception of themselves and their capabilities.

If you believe that you are not living in a way that reflects the kind of person you want to be, it is time to consider a quantum shift. Here's the plan. As usual, I'm going to walk you through the chapter's version of the ~ing Equation: the Quantum Shifting Equation. However, in this particular version of the Equation, you're going to focus most of your energy on the rethinking section of the Equation in an effort to get lined up for a quantum shift. Then I'll encourage you to step outside your comfort zone by accessing a new physical activity. By doing a new physical activity, you'll exercise new behavior and begin to perceive yourself in a different light. The Receiving step will guide you to create a whole new perception of yourself through your meditation. Your meditation will be followed by an ~ing write where you will retell your story with a more positive spin. Finally, I've added an additional tool to this

Equation: you will be encouraged to reread and retell your new story on a daily basis for thirty days. So open your mind and get ready to feel the earth shift beneath you!

Before you begin the Equation ask yourself the following questions: *Is it a bird? Is it a plane? What kind of person do you want to be? What do you want to accomplish? How do you want to perceive yourself?*

After identifying who you want to be, answer the next question: *Is who you want to be much different from who you are today?*

If it is, think about what it is that you are doing that is causing this disconnect. For instance, if what you want to be is a success in your career, are you still going out and partying every night, only to show up at work the next day with a major hangover that causes you to perform at half your capacity? Or if you want to be a good friend, do you tend to drop your friends the minute you get a boyfriend? Or if you want to be a eco-conscious citizen of the world, are you doing anything toward that end?

THE QUANTUM SHIFT*ing* EQUATION
—Thirty Days to a New You

STEP ONE: Rethink*ing*

Open your mind. Being open to the idea that change is within reach is a key element in this process. Have faith in the stories related above and know that you have the same capacity to change your perception of yourself that anyone has. Follow these steps:

Step 1: Get Honest

Are you stuck accepting a negative perception of yourself?

What is your current story of yourself? Write it out.

How have you been blocking yourself from being the person you want to be and achieving the things you want to achieve?

How does the world mirror any negative perceptions you have of yourself?

Step 2: Rethink

Take your answers to the above questions and revise them to fall in line with the person you want to be. Follow the guide below:

- Tool One: Get unstuck. If you are stuck in a negative perception of yourself, change that negative perception to a positive one. For instance, if you answered: *I am unmotivated, lazy and unfocused*, change it to: *I am ambitious, highly motivated, hard working and focused.*
- Tool Two: Rethink your current story. Change it to reflect the story of who you want to be.
- Tool Three: Bulldoze your blocks. For example, if you answered, *I block myself from playing music professionally because I fear that I won't be able to make money*, rewrite it as, *I am actively pursuing my music career and I make tons of money doing it.*
- Tool Four: Reverse how others respond to you. How would you like the world to perceive you? Rewrite the script of how others react to you. For example, if your parents do

not support your desire to play music professionally, write out, *My parents fully support my desire to play music and they show up to every gig.*

Step 3: Disengage

When your thoughts and feelings are still aligned with fear and negativity, the people in your life will reflect that back to you. Don't let others hold you back from experiencing a quantum moment. Practice disengaging. Identify the people in your life who fuel your fear. Forgive them, because they are merely a reflection of your inner beliefs. Then disengage. The *Course* says that "Insistence means investment." This lesson teaches that when we insist on engaging in other people's fear we are investing in it. In addition, if we attack their fear with a defensive attitude, we are still investing in it. Instead, forgive them and move on. Stop engaging in the negative perceptions of the world; it only blocks your change.

STEP THREE: Rethinking + Moving

In this version of the Equation, I'm going to ask that you do something physical that is totally out of your comfort zone. It could be as wild as bungee jumping, trapeze flying or skydiving, or it could be as simple as taking a dance class. What's important is to do something that you would never perceive yourself doing. Go out and experience an activity that you've always wanted to do but were too afraid to try.

By taking action to step outside your comfort zone, you are creating a new perception of yourself. You will experience a sense of pride. You will be psyched that you tried something new, and you will have a cool story to tell. Most importantly, you will begin to see yourself as someone who is willing to do new things—someone who is willing to experience a quantum shift.

STEP THREE: Receiving (Meditating/~ing write)

Vision Meditation

This meditation will be slightly different than the previous meditations I have walked you through. This one is dedicated to holding a vision of living in a new way. See yourself doing exactly what you truly want to do and being exactly who you want to be. Envision yourself set free from your negative perceptions. Create an entire scene around this vision. Witness how the world mirrors your happiness and flow. Invite other people into your visualization. Envision others vibrationally aligned with your truth and perfectly mirroring your new perception of yourself. Allow yourself to sit in this vision long enough to experience an emotional reaction of some kind. It might take a while, but it's well worth the wait. You may simply smile. Or possibly cry. Just let your emotions flow with the beautiful vision you create in your mind.

~ing write and Change Your Story

Now is your opportunity to rewrite the story of who you perceive yourself to be. Look closely at the story you've created of yourself. Identify where and how you've been sabotaging the goal of becoming the person you want to be. Listen to your *inner guide* and for ten minutes *~ing write* your new story. Use images or sensations from your meditation to guide you as you write. Be specific about what kind of person you want to be and what actions you need to take to get there.

Create Your Personal-Shift Statement

When you finish ~*ing writing,* immediately reread what you wrote. Underline the sentences that ignite a passionate feeling in you. Then extract those sentences from the page and put them together in paragraph form. Ideally you will pull two or three sentences. Next, edit down the paragraph so it reads like a personal statement. Reread it and check in with how it makes you feel. If the statement embodies your idea of who you want to be, then you've successfully created a personal-shift statement.

An example of a personal shift statement sounds like this:

I am a professional singer. I go on tour monthly and am paid very well for my work. My singing career is beautifully aligned with my personal life.

STEP FOUR: Rereading & Retelling

The final step in this equation is to actively reread and retell. Every night for the next thirty days, reread your personal statement. Allow your mind to guide your emotions into vibrational alignment with your new perception of yourself. Experience your new and improved self on a nightly basis, and enjoy how it feels to be her or him.

Share your personal statement at least once a day, for thirty days, with someone else. Feel free to tell complete strangers the story as if it is already happening. It may sound like I'm asking you to lie, but in fact it's the exact opposite. What I'm asking you to do is to act as if you are already there so that your mind will catch up with your personal-shift statement. When your mind does catch up, the quantum shift will occur.

In the upcoming chapter you'll be guided to further enhance the shifting process with the practice of focusing your own energy. Begin to turn your desire into reality with the Focusing Equation.

CHAPTER
NINE

*Focusing: Tuning Your
Energy to a Positive
Frequency*

Perception has a focus. It is this that gives consistency to what you see.
Change but this focus, and what you behold will change accordingly.

—A Course in Miracles

Claire lived in a constant state of chaos as a result of her desire to control the outcome of every situation. She obsessed over every detail of her life, whether it was the outcome of a job interview or a date she'd had the night before. This constant obsessing only led to drama and an overall feeling of anxiety. Each morning Claire awoke with the pang of fear in her chest. On top of that, she had a nasty case of the "when I haves," always deferring her happiness for "when I have [insert desire of the month here]." Despite these tendencies, Claire was an upbeat, outgoing young woman. But it was clear that her obsessive nature and her need to control every detail of her life were blocking her happiness.

One afternoon Claire sent me a text saying, "Call me ASAP." I called her right away. She answered, saying, "I am freaking out! I can't stop thinking about this job I just interviewed for. I need a job so badly and I won't calm down until I know the outcome." "Slow your roll, sister," I responded. "All your worrying will get you nowhere. You never worry that the sun will rise, right?" Puzzled by my question, she replied, "No, never." I said, "If you have faith that the sun will rise, why don't you have faith that you'll get a job?" This comment made no sense to her. She laughed off my remark and bulldozed on with her fear talk about unemployment and the crappy job market. Finally, I cut her off and quoted the *Course:* "Do you want the problem, or do you want the answer?" "Of course I want the answer!" she replied. "Then it's time to let go of the rope," I said. "The answer comes when you refocus your thoughts and your energy to align with your ~*ing* rather than your ego." Finally she surrendered and said, "Fine! Show me what you got. Anything is better than this." This began her lesson in ~*ing* focused energy.

And that begins your lesson in ~*ing*-focused energy. In this chapter, I will show you how to align your thoughts with positive energy so that you can attract greatness. First I'll walk you through the common blocks that may be keeping your energy from attracting the positivity of the Universe. Then I'll show you the dangers of living with unfocused energy. Lastly, I'll walk you through the Focus*ing* Equation, which is designed to help you clean up the thoughts and feelings that block you from attracting.

The goal of this version of the ~*ing* Equation is to teach you how to focus the energy the Universe has allotted you every day of your life. And as a result, you will activate your energy positively and become a vibrational match for your focused desires. I'll guide you to change your energy and have faith in your attracting power. Your newfound faith will result in a super-cool way to live. It will surprise you how things will manifest when you focus your energy. Manifestation is the outward result of an inward intention. You manifest your desires into form by aligning your energy with powerfully focused thoughts and precise vision.

BLOCKS

You spend a lot of time worrying about things like whether you'll get a job or whether your date from last Friday will call back, but do you ever worry about something, like say, whether a magnet will attract iron, or if the needle on a compass will move? Hell no, you don't. Your worries are reserved for the areas of life that you have no faith in. Well, if you have faith in the energy that orbits the planets around the sun, why can't you have faith that your energy will help you get a job? The same energy that moves the planets is also moving inside you. You've just denied its capabilities.

Now that you realize that this same energy is inside of you, it's time to learn how to use it for good as opposed to what you have been unknowingly using it for. Because unbeknownst to you, you *have* been using this energy, just not to your advantage. As a result, your unfocused use of this energy has been attracting unfocused outcomes. It's also blocked you from receiving what you want.

For example, Martin wanted to leave his company and get a new job, but all of his focus was on his current crappy employer. So by focusing all of his energy on the job he hated, he was blocking himself from receiving new job leads. When he finally got up enough courage to leave the job he hated, he found himself in between employers for only two weeks, because with time to focus on his desires, he was able to revamp his energy. He was immediately happier because he was no longer in a place he despised. As a result of his focused, happy energy, within two weeks he landed a new job at a company he'd always wanted to work for.

Remember: like attracts like. Therefore, the energy that's vibrating inside you will bring similar energy to you. When you're vibrating on a super-cool frequency, then what comes your way will be equally as cool. But tuning your energy to your frequency of choice requires focus. Without proper focus you open yourself up to the random energy of the Universe. We are all magnets capable of attracting at all times. But your negative thoughts and feelings represent a brick wall that lies between you and all you are capable of attracting.

Your main block is that you don't know the power you have

over your energy. The *Course* reminds us, "The ego always speaks first. Its voice is always the loudest, and it is always wrong." Your ego tells you that you are a body that's separate from everything around you. The ego screams that you have to control everyone and everything in order to get what you want. The ego tells you to fear people, not to expect anything good out of life, and to worry about all outcomes. Identifying with this fear talk has deprived you of working with your *inner source of power*.

Another block is that, like Claire, you've become obsessed with future outcomes. Remember, the future and the past are pre-occupations of the ego. The only time that matters is right now. Fear of the future blocks you from enjoying the moment and co-creating with the Universe. For example, Jessica is completely freaked out about not finding a husband. She is totally caught up in the mentality of "when I have a husband, I'll be happy." Her fear of not finding "the one" has become her greatest block toward happiness and love. At parties her energy is anxious as she looks around the room for prospective suitors. When she meets a guy she finds attractive, her energy then turns needy. She acts as if he's the last man on earth, which is a total turnoff to any guy.

THE PITFALLS OF UNFOCUSED ENERGY

In addition to the blocks that might stop you from achieving all the positivity the Universe has in store, you might be suffering from an inability to focus the energy of the Universe that exists inside of you. Without clear focus, you're bound to manifest some funky stuff. If you're thinking, "I want a home near water," but you don't clarify *where* you want to live, you could very well end up freezing your ass off in Alaska (no offense to Alaska).

My friend Tim Morehouse, a U.S. Olympic fencer, experienced this type of unfocused attracting at the 2008 Bejing Olympic Games. For the three months leading up to the Games, Tim and his team had set their intention on winning a medal. In each practice they got together to focus on the medal. (Note: group focus is *super* powerful.) They talked about it often and held visions of triumph. Energized and ready to win, they began the competitions with great performances. They beat the world-champion Hungarians in round eight, and then they beat the world powerhouse, Russia, which qualified them for a gold medal. At this point, fear set in. The clarity and confidence that the team had had throughout the competition was now kicked to the curb. As a result of their egos' throw-down, they finished the competition with a silver medal, losing the gold to France. Upon reflecting on their performance, they realized that their focus was unclear from the beginning. They had spent months holding the vision of a medal, but they never specified its color. Their lack of focus blocked them from winning the gold.

Now that you know what is blocking your energy from attracting all the positivity that the Universe has in store for you, and the dangers of not focusing that energy, it's time for me to show you how you can refocus your thoughts, stop blocking your magnetic power and allow the energy of the Universe to be your guide. Focused energy can act as a road map. Surrender to this energy and you'll feel guided, even when you arrive at what at first seems like a detour. Just follow your focused energy and be open to the Universe's detours. When your energy is tuned in to a positive vibration, you can have faith that you're always being guided either toward your desires or to a detour that will bring you *something better.* Why waste any more time trying to navigate on your own?

Stop blocking yourself from golden opportunities and start focus*ing*. Start off simple. Choose a low-key area of your life to focus on for the next thirty days. Test-drive the Focus*ing* Equation with a desire you're not that attached to. Your lack of attachment will help you as you practice working with your energy. If you were to choose something more significant at this time you might get tripped up over the results. Therefore, keep it simple at the beginning.

You'll then be led to apply specific tools for focusing this desire further and forming a clear vision. This step is followed by developing your clear vision into further focus with physical activities that will activate your inner energy. Then you'll flow into a meditation, which will guide you to activate feelings of happiness. This meditation will show you how to shift your energy at any given moment. You will be led to do this meditation in the morning followed by an *~ing write* exercise. Each morning you will *~ing write* on how you want to focus your energy that day. Remember, if you dedicate thirty days to focus*ing*, you can learn how to positively tune your energy at any given time. The more *~ing* you add, the more powerful your energy will be. With clear vision and focus, you can stop controlling and start creating.

Why try to navigate through life without a road map or a GPS? Tap in to your *inner guide* and let the Universe help with your sense of direction. Check out how connected you are to your *inner energy. Do you think you need to control the outside world in order to make things happen in your life? Do you try to manipulate the outcome of situations? Are you unaware of the fact that you can use your own thoughts to inform your energy and therefore enhance your life?* If your answers reflect that you are controlling or manipulating outcomes of your life's circumstances, that's a sure sign that you're not focusing your *inner energy.* Embark on a thirty-day focus*ing* journey and line your energy up with the power of the Universe.

THE Focusing EQUATION—
Thirty Days to Positively Focus Your Energy

STEP ONE: Rethinking

Let's refocus your lens. The rethinking goal is to focus your thoughts with the voice of your ~ing rather than the voice of the ego. When your thoughts are aligned with ~ing, your energy is stronger. My ~ing buddy, wellness guru and acupuncturist Bianca Beldini, emphasizes the importance of refocusing your energy: "Negative thoughts block your energy. When energy is blocked it causes mental, spiritual and physical stagnation. Like a river that's been dammed, one must refocus the flow to allow unimpeded energy to move smoothly." The rethinking tools below will guide you to recreate your thoughts, replacing the ego's illusions with love. When you focus on loving thoughts, you create loving visions. The emphasis in this step is on perfecting your thought forms in order to strengthen your energy. Feel free to use your climbing exercise to help you reach for higher-level thoughts.

- Identify an issue that you want to refocus your energy around. For this first round, choose something that you're not too attached to. You might wish you had a better relationship with your boss, or maybe you'd like to redirect your energy around making new friends. Choose something that isn't too big for you to wrap your head around.
- Take note of how you currently feel when you focus on this situation or area of your life.
- What kinds of thoughts do you have about this situation or area of life?

Spot-Check Your Responses

Now that you've identified a simple area to work with, it's time to start changing your energy around it. The first step to changing your energy is to change your thoughts. So, say you want to focus on changing your energy around how you perceive money. Your thoughts have been saying, *I have trouble making money, I hate my job and I am always broke.* In that case you might write an affirmation such as: *Money flows to me with ease. I enjoy the work I do and I love receiving the financial benefits.*

Another example is that you may want to focus on a more positive way of living with your roommate because you often find yourself attacking her with negative thoughts. In that case your affirmation might read, *I forgive my roommate for past situations and I choose to enjoy our relationship today.* The key to these statements is to make sure you *feel* good about them. If for some reason the statement feels too far off for you, it might be tough for your ego to digest. If that's the case, you'll need to simplify the affirmation. Write out your new affirmation. Be sure to keep it powerfully aligned with loving thoughts that *feel* good to you.

STEP TWO: Rethinking + Moving

Focusing Your Mind and Your Energy

A great ~ing girl example of the power of focus is when I picked up a childhood hobby—unicycling. When I was twelve, I was enrolled in a circus arts program. I lived for it! I became obsessed with unicycling to the point where I made my father buy me one. But throughout adolescence I put down my hobby for fear of not being cool. Seventeen years later, I woke up to the realization that cool equaled unicycling! I was determined to rock out on one wheel. Much like riding a bike, your muscles remember the physical movements of unicycling. I didn't have too much trouble getting back on, though I clearly needed a lot of practice.

With a focused vision of my desire, I set out to make this goal a reality. I was to be a uncycling rockstar. Armed with a unicycle and an affirmation, I embarked on my focus*ing* journey. My affirmation was: *I am focused on my desire, I am an amazing unicyclist.* Thirty days of focus*ing* on this objective did the trick. By the end of the process I was riding with confidence.

The following activities have been chosen for this Equation because they help sharpen your focus. Suggested focus*ing* activities: running, unicycling, golfing, shooting hoops and archery. Although I've offered suggested activities, you can really apply any activity to the Focus*ing* Equation if it is foreign to your body. Practice focusing your thoughts to align with your energy so that you can achieve your desired goal. By mentally focusing while trying to master a physical action, you will align your mind and body to energize a new way of being.

Refocusing Your Energy

Oftentimes you may need to refocus your energy, and your mind might need some help. If that's the case strap on some sneakers and go for a run. Pay close attention to how the thoughts shift in your mind and how the energy shifts in your body. You may reach a place of white noise where all of your worries disappear. Refocus your energy by simply going for a run.

STEP THREE: Receiving (Meditating/~*ing* write)

Go to www.addmoreing.com and download my focus*ing* meditation or read below. This meditation will guide you to focus on positive thoughts and feelings in order to ignite powerful energy. Remember that in order to focus your energy in a positive way, you must *feel* positive. Repeat the focus*ing* meditation for thirty days.

Close your eyes and take a deep breath, in through your nose and out through your mouth. Hold a vision in your mind of a person, place or situation that makes you happy. Sit for a moment and let your mind create story angles and images that connect with this vision. As you breathe in, connect with the feelings of happiness that these visions ignite. As you exhale, release these happy thoughts into the Universe. Continue to breathe in joyful feelings and identify where they are held in your body. Breathe directly into that area of your body, accessing a closer connection to your feelings of joy. Notice your energy refocus from what you were feeling prior to a new state of joy. Feel the energy inside you vibrate as you exhale it out into the Universe. Practice enhancing this energy with each inhale. Share this energy with every exhale. Know that as you ignite this energy inside, it is positively affecting everything and everyone around you.

~ing write

For the next thirty days, *~ing write* in the morning. Free-flow your *~ing write* to focus on the energy you want to feel that day. Let your *inner guide* inform your words to describe the way you wish to feel. Creatively visualize yourself filled with this feeling. Write your way into the feelings. Create new powerful visions through your writing. Welcome the feelings that come forth as you write freely about your desired energy. Begin each day with this *~ing write* and magnetize your energy into a positive vibration.

Enjoy the results of focusing your energy. As soon as you experience the feeling of co-creating your energy with the Universe, you will be inspired to do it all the time. Keep focus*ing*.

The next crucial step in the manifestation process is know*ing* your desires are on the way. Chapter ten will teach you the simple Know*ing* Equation that with dedication and practice will lead you into "the know."

CHAPTER TEN

Knowing: The Universe Has Your Back

Those who are certain of the outcome can afford to wait and wait without anxiety.
—A Course in Miracles

Beliefs are removed. Believing is replaced with knowing.
—Your Sacred Self *by Dr. Wayne Dyer*

Recently, a client I coach asked me the difference between "wishing" and "knowing." I explained that the difference between the two is immeasurable. When you wish for something, your ego believes *you* can control the outcome. However, behind a wish is a sense of need, which leads to the emission of a grasping type of energy. In addition, when you're wishing for something to happen, you brace yourself for more than one kind of outcome. You wish for a thing to happen, but you prepare yourself to deal if it doesn't. With a wish, there is a lack of certainty. A wish can be perceived as a pipe dream that *might* come true. The uncertainty behind this thinking leads to fear that the thing you're wishing for won't actually come to fruition. You can repeat as many positive affirmations as you like, but if there is a sense of fear that what you're wishing for won't come to pass, then you're actually blocking yourself from receiving it.

Know*ing* is vastly different from wishing. When you're in a state of knowing, you are relaxed and your energy vibrates at a positive frequency. When your energy is in a good vibration, you *know* you are hooked up. When you get yourself to a place of know*ing* that whatever you desire is on the way, you *feel* it in your gut. You relax into the manifestation process (the "manifestation process" is simply the road map of why and how you get the results that you get in life; more on that to come) and *allow* your desires to flow to you like iron to a magnet. Time becomes irrelevant because you're enjoying the moment and have faith in the future. More importantly, you *know* that if your exact desire does not show up, it's because the Universal map has a detour that leads to something better.

In this chapter I will discuss the importance of embracing a state of know*ing*. In that vein, I'll show you what can happen if you're not in the know, and share with you how I was able to stay on my three-year path to know*ing*. Lastly, I'll introduce this chapter's ~*ing* Equation, the Know*ing* Equation, and tell you why this equation stands out from the pack.

MANIFESTATION MISHAPS

What blocks you from know*ing* is your lack of commitment to the energy of the Universe. Wishing and hoping are beautiful behaviors, but they must be transformed to complete know*ing* before you can fully receive. From time to time you may get close to specific desires that you "wanted" or "wished for," but without complete faith, you won't continue attracting success; you'll have *successful manifestations* followed by *ego-controlled situations.*

For instance, Nancy, a young woman I coach, needed to make $10,000 in one month for the real estate company she worked for. If she didn't earn that amount, she would lose her job. With fire under her ass, she put the manifestation process into action. She clarified her desire statement and focused her intentions. She began practicing the Focus*ing* Equation on a daily basis. She walked the walk and talked the talk, affirming daily, "I will make $10,000 for my company this month." Within two weeks she made the $10,000, and by the end of the month she had exceeded her goal by $5,000. She was thrilled with the results. The next month she decided to do it again. However, this time her ego butted in, saying, "That was just luck. You can't do it twice in a row." Thus, her uncertainty and fear sabotaged her second month's earnings. She made excuses for what went down, complaining of the poor real estate market and the economy. But the truth was that Nancy had relinquished her positive energy to the power of the ego, and therefore discredited her prior manifestation. Nancy had blocked herself from the potential of earning as much, if not more, in the second month because she succumbed to the ego's fear.

Following her manifestation mishap, Nancy came to me for help. I explained that the only step she was missing was fully embracing the energy of the Universe. The number one most important step in manifestation is to *know* your desire is on the way. All her wishing and wanting only led to receiving *sometimes*. "Wouldn't you rather hang out just *knowing* that everything will work out, be guided and receive?" I asked Nancy. "Of course I want that," she replied. "But I feel frustrated and blocked because I have no idea how to get there."

Sympathetic to her frustration, I gently explained how the Know*ing* Equation could catapult her faith and knowingness. I went into a full-blown ~*ing* girl sermon on the topic. Here's the gist of what I told Nancy: "True knowingness comes with daily dedication to your ~*ing*. The problem that arises for people is that they get into their ~*ing* work for a little while and then slowly slack off, allowing the ego to take over the steering wheel. I've witnessed many people get 'good' at their ~*ing* work for a few days, a few weeks, or even a few months. As a result, they began to enjoy all of the positive outcomes of their ~*ing* practice. But far too often, their ego gets crafty and finds its way back in."

The good news is there is a way to protect yourself from the ego's backlash, and live each day know*ing* that you're being guided. The key to this level of know*ing* is devoted ~*ing* practice. As you now know, one of the ultimate results of each and every ~*ing* Equation is a positive shift in perception. The more you shift your perception, the more miracles you'll chalk up, and the more miracles you've chalked up, the closer you will get to know*ing* that the Universe has your back.

The bottom line is: living in the *know* requires a lifelong commitment to your ~*ing*. Though you may not be in full faith today, you can begin moving in that direction right now. As the miracles keep piling up, you'll eventually come to live in the *know*. Until then, if you need help hanging in, repeat the Twelve Step slogan, which has helped so many keep their faith over the years: "Fake it till you make it." That's exactly what I did while I was on my path to my state of *knowing*. But, most importantly, I showed up for my ~*ing* on a daily basis for more than four years. Then the day came when I was able to separate from my ego and fully embrace my ~*ing*. Although there were many moments in between when I had clear signs of the power of the Universe, it took a lot of ~*ing* work and patience to get to the place where I just *know*.

For instance, I spent over three years know*ing* that I would get this book published. I had a desire to tell a story, and I knew there was a book in me. Once I signed a manager to sell my book idea, I remained relaxed and at ease. I *knew* that the book would sell to just the right publisher at just the right time. In fact, my manager almost sold my book to a different publisher a year earlier. When that deal fell through, I *knew* it was because there was something better on the way. And in fact, it was way better! It was an entirely different book concept that was sold a year later.

Luckily for me, the Universe had a better plan and I was willing to let her do her thing. Patiently staying in the *know* is what led me to the right publisher at the exact right time. To stay in the rad vibration of know*ing*, I take daily action to maintain my faith by practicing the Know*ing* Equation.

PRAY*ing* + MEDITAT*ing* = KNOW*ing*

The key components of the Know*ing* Equation are pray*ing* and meditat*ing*. Praying is the time to ask and meditating is the time to listen. This is something I realized on my path to know*ing*. On a daily basis, I would set my intention each morning by saying a prayer to the Universe. In some cases I would fully surrender and even get on my knees. I didn't perceive this as religious or strange; it just made the whole praying experience more powerful. Getting down on my knees conveyed in a very physical way that I was ready to turn my will and my life over to the energy of the Universe.

Following my prayer, I sat in a minimum of a ten-minute meditation where I'd clear my mind and listen to my *inner guide*. As the weeks wore on, ten minutes became twenty, and twenty turned into an hour. Sometimes I'd meditate twice in one day. In my meditation I'd simply listen to my ~*ing*. I'd spot-check my feelings that day and allow my *inner guide* to reshape my thoughts from fear back to love. Some days I'd get super inspired and jump from my meditation to reading a book that had been sitting on my shelf for months. Other days I'd feel myself fully surrender to forgiv*ing* someone I'd been resenting. In some cases, I'd just sit in my meditation and calm my thoughts so that I could continue the day with ease and in a more positive, energetic state.

By taking daily action to pray and meditate, I was focusing on loving thoughts and energy while surrendering to my ~*ing*. As a result, I was led to specific people, situations and circumstances. The days that I woke up late and skipped my know*ing* ritual were days that felt off to me. Therefore I'd ~*ing* it up later in the day when I had the chance. I'd also take any opportunity to pray and meditate. If I couldn't do it in my apartment, I'd do it on the subway by turning on my iPod and shutting my eyes to listen. I'd pray and meditate before dates, business meetings, even before I went to the gym. I'd simply turn my desires over to the Universe and ask for guidance.

In the beginning, my prayers just seemed like words, and my meditations, silent sitting. In between, a miracle or two would crop up. But as the miracles began to pile up, I could no longer deny what was going on, and I began to have true faith that the Universe was on my side. With my new found sense of know*ing*, I felt a deeper connection to the Universe. It was as though I was in a relationship with something much larger than the world I could see. I felt guided. I no longer had to control and manipulate the outcome of situations and relationships. I no longer had to worry. I felt an overarching sense that *everything was gonna be alright.* By continuing my daily prayer and meditation practice, I maintain this state of know*ing*.

Then I began to apply this knowingness to my manifesting,

and that's when things became amazi*ng*. I witnessed firsthand how life always works out when you surrender to the Universe by praying and meditating. When things didn't work out how I'd planned, somehow they'd end up even better. Things were good, but instead of slacking, I revisited my mentor Erica's admonition: "When things get good, work even more." So I did just that. I have kept up a daily ritual with my knowi*ng* practice of praying and meditating. The days became months, the months turned into years, and now I'm chilli*ng* in faith and knowi*ng*.

I am proud to say that I live the majority of the time in full faith that the Universe has my back, and I actually welcome the infrequent ego moments because they keep me on my toes. I keep my ego on a tight leash and allow it to mirror any hidden wounds. Who'd have thought some simple prayers and silent moments would lead to a life this good?

APPLYi*ng* THE KNOWi*ng* EQUATION

With only two steps, praying and meditating, the Knowing Equation is a bit of a departure from the other ~*ing* Equations. In addition, the Knowi*ng* Equation lacks a physical component. The reason for the difference is that this Equation is designed for a different type of endgame. Whereas all of the other equations are designed to change something specific in your life, the Knowi*ng* Equation is a constant, forever equation meant to keep you in the *know*. Praying and meditating are the two steps that will keep you always in a state of knowi*ng*. Another reason the Knowi*ng* Equation is more streamlined is to emphasize that staying in faith is not such a big deal. It just takes two simple daily actions: pray and meditate. Praying and meditating is what keeps you in constant contact with your ~ing, and it's that constant contact that keeps you in the know.

Another reason I've kept this ~ing Equation pocket-sized is that I'm extending the time frame. Rather than thirty days, your timeline for this equation is, well, forever. But, don't be intimidated; there are many types of prayer and meditation you can infuse into your life, and they're all super easy to do. In fact, until you get sick of listening to my voice, my meditations that will be available to you on www.addmoreing.com will keep you guided for a long time. As you practice your Knowing Equation, I'm asking that you keep it simple and steady. Stay on course and don't get tripped up in the details.

Below, I will guide you through the two simple steps of this equation and give you some easy examples of how to use this practice every day of your life. It doesn't matter how many books you've read, how many lectures you've attended or how long you've been in therapy. If you don't have a daily prayer and meditation practice, you're not furthering your faith. Start by asking yourself the question, "Did I pray and meditate today?" It's not about what you did yesterday or what you plan to do tomorrow. It's about what you do today.

First, I would like you to identify how you are struggling to stay on your path to truly, 100 percent in your heart and soul, knowing that the Universe is taking care of you. Please ask yourself the following questions: *When you set your intentions, do you have faith that the Universe is working to bring the best manifestation of them to you? Do you struggle to embrace the certainty of your desires coming to pass? Do you live in a constant state of fear that all the things that you want from the Universe will never come to pass? Do you get frustrated when life doesn't happen on your time frame? Are you having a hard time believing that the Universe will take care of you?*

THE KNOWI*ng* EQUATION—
Thirty Days to Knowing the Universe Has Your Back

STEP ONE: Praying

Remember that prayer is a time to ask. The first step in the pray-ing process is to clarify what you're asking the Universe for. In some cases, you may just be asking for the Universe to guide you to release your fears and live in faith. In other cases, you may be asking for something specific, like help with a health condition or a romantic relationships. Whatever the case may be, clarity comes first.

Clarify Your Request to the Universe

When clarifying your request, there are two important compo-nents. The first is to clarify the intention behind your desire, and the second is to clarify the way in which you're asking. When ad-dressing the intentions behind your desires, you want to be sure that you are not coming from a place of lack or neediness. When you're feeling needy, your energy is needy, and therefore you're far from a place of knowi*ng*. Furthermore, it's important that your in-tentions are aligned with the greater good.

When I speak of the "greater good," I mean that the desire is of service to others and the world in some way. For example, Sara's desire was to get married. She reprocessed the intention of her de-sire from *"I need a man to feel safe"* to *"I desire a husband because I will be an amazing mother and share my wisdom with my family."* This shift in per-ception is the difference between a needy request and an offering to the Universe. Your *inner guidance* does not run on *"how can I get?"* mode, but rather *"how can I give?"* mode. It's that "giving" energy that the positive energy of the Universe responds to.

Another example is Micaela's desire to be a fashion designer. At first you might think, "How can a fashion designer serve the world?" This is an easy answer. The reason her desire is of service to the world is because her mission is to heal through her designs. She has a story to tell through her work, and she *knows* that this story is aligned with the greater good. This makes her desire a powerful vibration for attracting greatness. Her inspiration for this desire is Donna Karan and her line "Urban Zen." The "Urban Zen" mission is to raise awareness and inspire change in conjunction with totally rockin' clothing. This power of example fuels Micaela's desires daily. Jessica is another example. Her desire is to be famous for her work as a yoga instructor. But, rather than backing her intention with a need for fame to make her feel good, she chose to pursue fame as a catalyst for sharing a healing message.

When your desires are backed with loving intentions of the greater good, you will feel the presence of an inner knowledge that you're on the right track and everything is lined up. So let's spot-check your desire or desires to clarify what the intention is behind them. To do so, ask yourself the following question and write out each answer.

How will your desire affect the world? (Note: you don't have to be saving lives to powerfully align your desires.)

This is what my statement might look like:

My desire is to be a best-selling author. This desire is aligned with the greater good because my books help people be happier.

Now you try it. Write out, *My desire is* _____.
This desire is aligned with the greater good because _____.

Check How You're Asking

To further align your asking prayer, let's take a close look at how you're communicating with the Universe. For example, I ran into a friend on the street and got to talking about a job that she'd been manifesting. She said to me, "Gab, I'm praying like crazy, but the damn Universe isn't responding!" I replied, "Would you respond if someone was talking to you with that kind of impatient attitude?" Remember that communicating with the Universe is less about what you think and say and all about the energy behind your feelings. Your feelings create your energetic vibrations, and that's what the Universe can respond to. Therefore, it's really important to clean up the energy behind *how* you're asking. Understand that the energy behind your prayers will shift when you release them to the Universe. To help you learn how to release your desires to the Universe, I give you the following tips on prayer.

- Pray*ing* Tip 1: Turn your prayers over to the Universe. In whatever way feels right for you, allow yourself to fully offer your desires to the Universe. One way to start could be by praying on your knees. When you physically show yourself and the Universe you're ready for help, the energy inside you shifts. Another way of expressing this release is to just say it. Simply say out loud, "I offer this desire to the Universe. I know it is being taken care of." Remember, "fake it till you make it." You might not be ready to turn it all over today, but simply start by saying it out loud or kneeling. These actions offer the Universe a powerful message that you are willing to let go of controlling the outcome.

- Pray*ing* Tip 2: Create a belief box. A belief box is a space that will hold your prayers. Decorate your box any way you like. Then simply write your prayer on a piece of paper and place it in the box. The act of putting it into the box conveys to the Universe that you are giving it away, and you *know* that it's being take care of.

- Pray*ing* Tip 3: Gratitude is the only attitude. Make a list of everything in your life that you are grateful for. Begin your morning prayer by reading your gratitude list out loud. This action is very powerful because it immediately aligns your thoughts and energy with love. This powerful energy will totally back up your prayers and set you up for the day.
- Pray*ing* Tip 4: Healing Prayers. My West Coast ~*ing* buddy psychotherapist, brain and body specialist, Dr. Erica Ellis, is all for using prayer as a healing tool. Erica says, "Research has demonstrated that prayer has a profound physiological effect on healing, including regulating cardiovascular activity, improving immune function and an overall decrease in stress levels. It may be that prayer helps to regulate your heart and signals to your body and brain that it is safe to relax and experience love. This suggests that by sending love and prayer to someone else, you may reap the same benefits as if you were sending love and prayer to yourself. In this way, prayer is really a one-two punch spiritual practice, further dissolving the traditional barriers between self and other."

Finally, treat the Universe like a best friend that wants to help you in all areas of your life. Fearlessly ask for guidance and direction. Align your requests with the greater good and lovingly ask the Universe for help. Trust me, she will listen.

STEP TWO: Meditat*ing*

The final step in know*ing* your life is taken care of is through a disciplined meditation practice. Meditation is dedicated time to spend with your *inner guide* in peace and silence. A daily commitment to meditation will give you an overall feeling of connection to the Universe, which in turn leads you to a state of know*ing* you are in alignment with your desires. Throughout the day you are typically in a brain frequency called "beta." The beta frequency is great for daily tasks and getting stuff done, but it's not contributing to your connection with the Universe. When you sit in a meditative state your brain literally switches frequencies. As you allow yourself to be guided by my voice and release your tension, your brain is led into an alpha brain wave frequency, a lower-frequency brain wave that calms your mind. In this calm frequency you are relaxed enough to let loose your desires to the quantum field of possibility. Outlined below are a few examples of how meditation will guide you into further knowingness and co-creation with the Universe.

Meditative Visions

By calming your beta frequency and relaxing into your alpha frequency, you will be guided to create visions and release plans. There is a major difference between a vision and a plan. The plan is all about controlling an outcome whereas a vision is a loving contemplation. When in your meditation work, you will create visions that are wrapped with loving intentions. You create these visions by offering your desires to your ~*ing* during meditation. Simply hold an idea of something you desire in your mind and offer it to your ~*ing* in meditation. When you are in the midst of your meditation, your brain is in the alpha state and therefore super creative.

This is when your ~*ing* can get to work. When your mind is

still it can receive guidance from your ~ing and flow creatively into supercool visions. For example, Jessica envisioned herself teaching yoga at the leading institutes in the country. In her vision, she saw loving light pour off of her body. This represented her healing influence on the world. Jessica's vision of sharing her light with the masses not only served her happiness, but spread joy energetically throughout the ether. She was then able to release her plans and focus on the love behind her intentions. Her ~ing meditation reminded her that love breeds love. By creating this loving vision daily in her meditation practice, Jessica was guided to teach yoga in front of larger and larger classrooms and spread her healing light.

White Light Meditations

I heard another powerful example from two co-authors who were trying to find a publisher for their book. For several weeks they used the power of visualization to make this desire a reality. They sat in meditation and envisioned white light piercing into the book, saying *"Publish me!"* They dedicated time to this meditation daily. Three weeks later they received a call from a publisher. He said, "I never publish books like this, and it's completely not my beat. But this book keeps screaming, 'PUBLISH ME!'" They signed a publishing agreement soon after.

An additional step not to be missed is to *feel* the feelings behind your desires. For instance, Sara manifested her desire for a husband through her feeling meditations. She did walking meditations throughout the streets of New York City, embodied with the *feeling* of being in love. Each night before she went to sleep she envisioned what he looked like, how he moved and how he made her *feel*. In her meditation she sent white light from her heart to his heart. She woke each morning having dreamed beautiful dreams of their time spent together and shared love. Most importantly, she paid close attention to the way he made her *feel*. She lived in the knowledge that each day that they were apart, he was preparing himself for her. In that time she witnessed many miracles. Men would stop her on the street to ask for her number. Each night of the week, she had a date with a different man. Her energy was vibrating a loving frequency out to the Universe, and men were vibing with it. Within two months she met Peter, who was the embodiment of her visions. They've been together ever since.

Your desires are prayers. When you bring your positive energy into alignment with your desire, you will *know* the delight of the answered prayer. To think it. To feel it. To know it.

WHITE LIGHT MEDITATION: (AUDIO AVAILABLE ON WWW.ADDMOREING.COM.)

Close your eyes. Take a deep breath in through your nose and exhale out through your mouth.

Breathe in—I wrap my intentions with love.

Breathe out—I am grateful.

Breathe in—I align my desires with the greater good.

Breathe out—I know I'm being guided.

Breathe in—I wrap my intentions with love.

Breathe out—I am grateful.

Breathe in—I align my desires with the greater good.

Breathe out—I know I'm being guided.

Hold a vision in your mind of what you desire. See yourself holding space in this vision with white light pouring off of you. Know that this white light represents the loving intention behind your desire. Send love from your heart into the ether. Know that this loving vibration is what is attracting your desires. Envision white light pouring into the object of your desire. This piercing white light holds all of the love of the universe. This white light represents your intentions and aligns your energy with life's flow.

The *Course* teaches us that five minutes spent in prayer or meditation with your *inner guide* in the morning will guarantee that your thoughts will be aligned with love throughout the day. Know that your inner alignment will create miracles. Begin each day with this mantra: *I believe. I choose love. I co-create with the Universe. My inner guidance leads me. I choose love and receive love.*

Thirty days spent in the Know*ing* Equation will line you right up for what's to come in chapter eleven. With your positively aligned focus and a true inner knowingness, you're ready to begin manifesti*ng*.

CHAPTER ELEVEN

Manifesting: Co-Create with the Universe

Miracles occur naturally as expressions of love.

—A Course in Miracles

Courtney had been coaching with me for more than five months. Her *inner light* was on. Eager to move forward she said, "I'm ready to start manifesting." I too believed she was ready, and agreed to teach her the Manifes*ting* Equation. I began by explaining that manifestation is the outward result of an inward intention. The process of manifesting your desires into form requires activating your energy with powerfully focused thoughts and precise vision.

Courtney was ready for this process because she'd successfully used the Focus*ing* Equation to consciously align her thoughts with positive intentions. In addition, she had just finished up a thirty-day Know*ing* Equation where she activated her daily conversation with the Universe though prayer and meditation. It was now time for Courtney to take her belief system a few steps further with the Manifes*ting* Equation.

To simplify my lesson, I stuck to what she knew best. Courtney was on the varsity archery team at her college. She had been archery shooting since she was twelve years old. Luckily for me, this sport happens to be a genius metaphor for manifesting. I went step by step, breaking down the components of manifesting through the eyes of an archer. I began with the first step in the manifestation process, which is focus. As any good archer knows, your *focus* must be sharply aligned with the "ten." (Courtney had taught me that the ten is the little "x" in the middle circle of the target board.) The next step is to make sure you are *calm*. If your energy is frenzied, your arrow will be wobbly. Once you've aligned your focused desire with calm energy, you are ready to *release* the arrow. As you release your arrow, you *know* that it will hit the ten. Finally, if you don't hit the ten in the first shot, you remain *patient* that your shot that will hit the ten is coming soon.

Courtney was diggin' my metaphor and was ready to learn the steps of the Manifest*ing* Equation. Like Courtney, I believe by this point in our journey together that you are also ready to learn the Manifest*ing* Equation. But before I begin taking you step by step through the equation, I would first like to rev you up with some powerful examples of successful manifestations. My memory bank is loaded with countless manifestation miracles; however, the ones I've chosen to share with you here best convey the importance of the three major elements of the Manifest*ing* Equation—focusing, releasing, and knowing.

Focus*ing*

One of the many reasons I chose to work with my coach Rha is because she is a manifesting maven. She had everything I wanted in all areas of her life. (Note: when people have what you want, do what they do.) Everything she had was a result of her dedication to her *inner guide* and her perfected manifestation practice. She has the manifesting method down to a science. One of Rha's manifestation stories that really inspired me was how she attracted her husband, Corey. She MANifested eighty-two of the eighty-four items on her "husband" list. That's right. She made a list of all of the qualities she wanted in a husband and manifested nearly all of them.

When I heard her story, I said, "Sign me up and show me the way!" She began by teaching me the importance of *focus*. She would often say, "It's not what you deserve, it's what you want."

Rha was not afraid to ask for what she wanted, hence the eighty-four items on her MANifestation list. She went on to teach me how she worked her manifesting process. She got super clear about what she wanted by itemizing her list. She labeled each quality either "non-negotiable," "superimportant," "really important" or "great." Then she wrote "him" a letter. This letter ignited the feelings of love and passion that she desired. She read this letter nightly and allowed herself to feel the joy of what it felt like to be with him. Her feelings guided her to a place of deep knowing that "he" was on the way. She shared her list with her friends and committed to her desires. By doing so, she figured, she would not end up wasting time dating men who didn't fit the bill. She used her meditation techniques and power of positive thinking to further focus her vision of her husband. Then she met Corey. When they first met, she didn't recognize that he could be "the one." He was an incredible guy, but she didn't consider him because he wasn't what she was "looking" for.

As time went on and they got to know each other, however, Rha got hip to the fact that Corey made her *feel* exactly how she wanted to feel. This was crucial. Corey embodied nearly everything on her list, except for two things. What had thrown Rha off from the beginning was the picture frame rather than the content. Corey was under six feet, and white. On Rha's list, her ideal man was tall and black. It was easy for Rha to throw these external credentials in the trash and embrace the greatness of the man she had attracted. They have been married ever since.

Rha's story is a powerful example of how when you shoot for the ten and hit the nine and a half, you can still be psyched with the outcome. The ten is what you should aim for, but often the Universe has an even better plan. So be focused on what you want, but remain open to the greatness of all possible outcomes.

RELEAS*ing*

As you know by now, when your thoughts are negative, your energy is lowered. Much of that low-level energy gets stuck in your precious body. Our bodies hold a great deal of guilt and sadness from our pasts—the old experiences we have not worked through. I held this stagnant energy in my jaw and vocal chords. Literally and metaphorically, I had something I *needed* to say. My unhealed feelings of not being heard had blocked my voice. By denying my inner voice, I not only became emotionally ill, but I also created a physical condition of vocal nodules which is like calluses on the vocal chords. My vocal chords were so damaged that doctors suggested I be silent for more than a month. The only alternative solution was a very dangerous surgery. This was clearly not an *~ing* Girl option.

Determined to find a better way, I turned to the guru of manifest*ing* health, Louise Hay. Her book, *You Can Heal Your Life*, has saved thousands of lives, including her own. Louise cured her cervical cancer through releasing fear, saying positive affirmations and practicing creative visualization. She knew that her cancer was a direct result of unhealed anger over being raped and battered as a child. With a past like that, it came as no surprise to her that she manifested cancer in her cervix.

Having been a teacher of manifesting healing, Louise knew that the Universe had given her this condition so she could use her methods on herself and share them with the world. Her belief system is: *"Disease can be reversed by simply reversing mental patterns."* Her cancer had manifested because she still harbored old resentments. With this clear understanding, she put her methods to work. By fearlessly forgiving people and situations from her past, she cured her emotional condition. Through affirmations and creative visualization, among other things, she further healed her physical condition.

If Louise could manifest her cure for cancer, I knew I could manifest healing my vocal chords. I stuck to her plan like glue. Louise's work taught me that my throat condition was, in her words, the result of "being unable to speak up for myself, swallowed anger, stifled creativity and refusal to change." Boy, was she right! I took my "medicine" daily by reciting the affirmation she designed for throat conditions: *"It's okay to make noise. I express myself freely and joyously. I speak up for myself with ease. I express my creativity. I am willing to change."* By *releasing* my past fears of speaking up and reciting her affirmations, my vocal chords began to strengthen. I then kicked my Manifest*ing* Equation into high gear by incorporating creative visualization, a form of meditation that allows your right brain to get to work. I would visualize white light pouring into my vocal chords. I'd inhale the white light and see it pour through me like water. With each inhalation, I saw my vocal chords getting stronger and stronger.

Gradually, the nodules disappeared. I repeated my Manifest*ing* Equation daily for thirty days. By the end of the month, I went to my doctor for a checkup. He took pictures of my vocal chords and was amazed to report that the nodules were no longer there. Shocked, he asked, "What have you been doing?" I replied, "Manifest*ing* my voice back." (Disclaimer: I am not suggesting that you substitute Western medicine or any other therapy for healing purposes, but I do suggest you add manifesting to your healing process.)

Knowing

Lora lost her job right before my New Year's lecture entitled "2009 is 2000MINE." The focus of the lecture was manifesting your desires in the coming year. Lora came to the lecture with a clear desire for a new job. She knew exactly what she was looking for and could speak about it with confidence. In fact, she did just that. Lora's hand shot up when I asked the audience for questions. She fearlessly announced to a room of more than eighty strangers that the only element she was missing in the Manifesting Equation was the *knowing* part. I encouraged her to release her desire to the Universe.

I led the group in a shared visualization of Lora getting the new job that she desired. As a group, we prayed for her new job and sent a powerful message to the Universe that she was ready to receive. (Note: Group prayer is super powerful. The power of collective thought creates a huge vibration of energy for the Universe to respond to.) After the lecture, I gave Lora some homework. I told her to ~*ing write* a letter to the Universe before she went to bed. In her letter she would release her desire to the Universe and expect a miracle. She took my advice and went home to write her letter.

The next day I received an e-mail from Lora. The subject read, "Expect miracles!" Her excitement shimmered off the computer screen as she told me about her manifestation. That morning she'd received notice that she got a job she'd applied for a week earlier. This was not just any old job. It was *the* job she had been manifesting! Lora was psyched to say the least. Her focus, commitment and shared belief were what the Universe responded to. Her energy was aligned with her desire, and most importantly, she expected a miracle. Her knowingness was what completed her manifestation.

CO-CREATE WITH THE UNIVERSE

Allow these manifestation miracles to inspire you to start co-creating with the Universe. Now, I'd like to give you a general overview of the equation before I guide you through its steps. The first step in the Manifest*ing* Equation is to clarify your desire. Clarity is crucial because you want to make sure you call in exactly what you want. When your focus is unclear, you get unclear results. Therefore the rethink*ing* step will guide your clarity when you create a powerfully focused desire statement. This statement will become an integral part of the Manifest*ing* Equation. You will then bring your desire statement with you into a meditation. In the meditat*ing* step, I will guide you into further focus by asking you to begin visualizing your desire. Meditat*ing* is the time when your brain softens and your energy becomes aligned with the energy frequency of the Universe.

The next step is to ~*ing write*. In this ~*ing write*, you will be led to relinquish your desire to the Universe through a written prayer. This prayer will act as a tool to help get in you in the *know*. Next, in the mov*ing* step, you will bring your desire statement with you on an outdoor physical adventure. The goal is to share your desires with the earth. For instance, you'll recite your desire statement as you hike up a mountain, run in the woods or swim in the ocean. You'll ~*ing* with your desires outdoors and let your energy and intentions connect with the earth around you. This step will help ground you into your desires and use the energy of the earth to add to your Manifesting Equation.

You'll finish the Equation off with the chilling step. The importance of chilling is that in order to receive your desires, you must be patient. As it says in the *Course*, "Only infinite patience produces immediate results." You'll see it when you believe, so just chill out, relax and receive it.

Finally, before I throw down the Manifesting Equation, let me remind you of some possible ways you might block your magnetic energy. I'd hate for you to do all this work and unconsciously be blocking the natural flow of the Universe! The first block to be aware of is fear or doubt. If fear or doubt sets in, revisit the Knowing Equation and realign your energy with your desired beliefs. Another thing that can block you is jealousy. Be aware of any jealous attacks you throw onto others. Instead of being jealous of others, start appreciating who they are and what they have. One of the key elements to manifesting is appreciating. By appreciating greatness, you create more opportunities to attract it in your life.

Finally, a major block toward manifesting your desires is impatience. Being patient is crucial to the manifesting process. Far too often I find that people block themselves from receiving because their ego gets impatient, telling them that they will never get what they want. I address this block further in the final step of the equation.

In order to enjoy the process of manifesting, it is imperative that you allow yourself to be unapologetic about what you want. Most importantly, you must allow yourself to *want*, period. Your ego has trained you to think that life's tough and you have to struggle to get what you want. Well, as usual, the ego is wrong. When you learn to powerfully co-create with the Universe, you can take pleasure in wanting and receiving. Make a list of two or three things you want to manifest. You can choose to manifest anything you desire. Do you want to attract a soul mate, a new job, a great new apartment? Make a desire list.

THE MANIFESTing EQUATION—
Thirty Days to Manifesting Your Desires

STEP ONE: Rethinking

Focus, Focus, Focus

This step is all about getting super focused on what you're ready to manifest. First, begin by identifying the one thing you want to manifest. Eventually you'll be able to manifest more than one thing at a time, but if you're a first-timer let's stay focused on one desire. Some examples include manifesting a new job, a new relationship, an apartment, better health, etc. In some cases you might just want to manifest a better social life.

A key element to deciding what to manifest is being honest with yourself about why you want it. Remember, if your desires are aligned with negative energy or an overarching feeling of "when I have that, then I'll be happy," you'll need to revisit your intentions. If your feelings around your desire are negative or needy, the Universe will have trouble responding to that vibration. Therefore, choose something that *feels* good to you. In addition, be careful not to choose something that is too far to reach. For instance, Lisa wanted to make more money. When she set her intention, she first stated to the Universe that she wanted to triple her current salary. This desire got her ego pumping. Because she didn't *feel* aligned with the desire, her ego picked up on her internal fear of not being able to get that amount. Therefore, Lisa continued to struggle to make more money because no matter how much she *thought* she wanted it, she didn't *feel* she could receive that amount. While it's super cool to think big, make sure your big ideas don't trigger fear. If your desires make you feel uneasy in any way, this is a sure sign that you need to realign the desire.

Now it's time to become even more focused about what you desire. For example, if you want a new job, make a list of how the job makes you *feel* and what it has to offer. For instance, "I have a desk next to a window, my boss treats me very well, I have health insurance, I feel safe to share my creative thoughts and ideas." Be very specific with this list. Remember, Rha had eighty-four items on her MANifestation list. She was not playing small. Be unapologetic about your desires and make sure you feel good about them when you list them out.

Clearly Define Your Desires

Following your list, write a statement clearly defining your desire. For example, Lora's desire statement looked like this: "I desire a new job working in travel public relations. My salary has doubled and I love my work environment. My work is of service to the world because I am helping people learn more about new cultures." Note that she included how her desire was of service to the greater good. Don't forget that when your desire is aligned with the greater good, the Universe will be vibing with it.

Now it's time to post your desire statement everywhere. Put it on your fridge, on your mirror, on your computer, etc. Make it a point to look at your statement as often as possible in order to reiterate your desire. Anyone who has been in my bathroom knows that I am a desire-statement fanatic. For over two years, both of my bathroom mirrors had written on them, "I am a published author." Guess what? It worked!

Share with Those Who Care

Next, it's time to reread and share your desire statement for the next thirty days. Read your statement at night before you go to bed. Hopefully the words will ignite a feeling inside you that will send off positive vibrations to the Universe. Then, each day, create more positive energy around your desires by sharing them with others. Connect with your power posse of friends who dig your new manifesting tools, and share your statement with them. If they support you, they will support your dreams.

Visioning

Focus your desires even further with a vision board. Vision boards are spaces for images that honor your desires. You can use a corkboard, canvas or even a magnet board. Post images, lyrics, quotes—anything at all that makes you feel aligned with your desire. For example, if you want to focus your energy around attracting a husband, post images of wedding rings, happy couples, wedding invitations, etc. Make sure that the images you post ignite a *feeling* of happiness in you.

My vision boards hold images such as magazines I plan to be featured in, a cutout image of Oprah next to an image of myself, surfboards and engagement rings. I can't begin to tell you how often my vision board comes to life. Each time I look at the images I reignite the focused energy in me that then sends messages out into the ether. I once received an e-mail from the *Huffington Post* asking me to be a blogger on their site. I wrote back, "Thanks for writing, I've been waiting for this e-mail." The *Huffington Post* logo had been on my vision board for more than two years. Stuff like this happens all the time! Add a new image to your board once a day for the next thirty days.

STEP TWO: Receiving (Meditating/~ing write)

In manifesting, meditation will invite the Universe into the process. I've included a morning meditation for creating and an evening meditation for thanking. By honoring the Universe for allowing you to be a co-creator, you are enhancing your connected energy and therefore amplifying your attracting power.

Morning Meditation

A morning meditation will really hook up your day and connect you to your energy from the onset. By setting your desired intention the moment you wake, you are enhancing your attracting potential and making a powerful statement to the Universe. Not only will your day flow with more ease, you will also activate your desire. Your morning requests will be picked up out in the ether. For the next thirty days, enjoy a morning manifestation meditation to jump-start your co-creation. Here goes:

As soon as you wake, sit up in your bed. Close your eyes and take a deep breath in through your nose and breathe out through your mouth.

Thank the Universe for another beautiful day.

Choose to align your thoughts and desires with the love of your inner guide.

Speak your desire statement out loud.

Thank the Universe for taking care of this desire and guiding you toward your visions.

Hold the vision of your desire in your mind. See it clearly.

Envision white light pouring into it.

See the white light continue pouring into the desire as you relax into the vision.

Sit in this vision for at least five minutes.

When you are finished, thank the Universe again and say, "I release this to the Universe and I know I will be guided."

Evening Meditation

Meditating before you sleep will help guide you into a peaceful state and ensure that you have a more restful night. A nighttime manifestation meditation is also an optimal opportunity to thank the Universe for the abundance it has brought forth throughout the day. Use this time to connect with feelings of gratitude and appreciation for everything you currently have and your desires that are on the way.

For the next thirty days, before you lay down to rest, sit up in your bed and follow this meditation.

Thank you, Universe, for the guidance and love you have provided me today.

Thank you for taking my desires and manifesting them into form.

Thank you for guiding my thoughts to loving perceptions and keeping my energy aligned with my visions.

I have gratitude for this beautiful day, and as I rest I release my desires to you.

Say your desire out loud and envision it in your mind.

I know this desire is on the way, and I welcome it in the best possible form.

It's either this or something better.

I will receive.

~ing write

Following your morning meditation, ~ing write for five minutes. Once again, release your desire into the Universe through this free write. Allow yourself to get honest in the writing about any impatient or possibly negative feelings or thoughts that come up. Use this writing exercise to clean up any negative energy from the day. This way you can be sure that your attracting power is on point and energetically aligned with the greater good. ~Ing write your way to a peaceful state of mind, and once again relinquish your desire to the Universe.

By releasing your desires through meditation and ~ing writing, you are getting yourself into the state of knowing that everything you want is on the way. It's important that you stick to the thirty-day release in order to maintain that positive flow of energy.

STEP THREE: Rethinking + Moving

Get outside and start moving. By moving outdoors, you're grounding your energy with the earth as you co-create your desires. Choose an activity that allows you to really connect with the earth. Go for a hike in the mountains, run in a park, swim in a lake or in the ocean. Surfing is an ~ing girl fave. If you can access the ocean, a surfboard, and an ~ing buddy who has surfed before, hit up some waves! (Make sure to go surfing with someone who knows what they're doing and can watch out for you.)

I became friends with surf guru Bill Hamilton (father of surfing legend Laird Hamilton) when I was in Hawaii. Bill's love for surfing has a lot to do with the magnetic energy he feels while spending time in the ocean. Bill says, "Spending my lifetime surfing in the ocean has made me like a magnet. I believe that I have taken in so much positive energy from the ocean that inevitably I draw in more positive people and positive experiences. Surfing is magnetizing." This insight from Bill drives home the message that moving with the energy of the earth truly activates your inner magnet. It also gets your endorphins pumping and your happy vibes flowing. Happy vibes equals positive attracting. When you feel your energy lift, you will notice that your life's circumstances become richer, and as a result you attract awesomeness. Remember that the key to attracting is aligning your energy with your desires, so don't take this step lightly. If you are truly ready to call in some greatness, go outside and get moving.

STEP FOUR: Chilling

An ~ing mentor of mine, Brooke Emory, the founder of The Attraction Boutique, is a power manifester. Brooke says, "Sometimes people will say, 'But why hasn't it happened yet?' By saying that, you take away your creation. And that's called mis-creation." Brooke's got that right! Patience is one of the most crucial components of the manifestation process. Therefore, I've included chilling in this equation for a very important reason. I would hate for you to do all the manifesting work and then block yourself from attracting by not having patience. Patience is by far one of the most important rules in manifestation.

For example, Jessica did a killer job following her manifesting guidelines. She got herself to a place where she really knew her desire of a boyfriend was on the way. Then her friends all started getting engaged. By watching her friends get hooked up, she went into panic mode and threw her ~ing out the window. She became incredibly impatient about when and how she was going to meet her man. This energy became a major block toward attracting. In the hopes of calming her down, I offered her a tool that would chill her out. I reminded her that the Universe is like her best girlfriend.

I asked her if she would ever pressure any of her girlfriends to find her a boyfriend. She replied, "No." Then I asked her whether or not her girlfriends wanted her to find true love, and if they were truly out to help her. She said, "Of course they are out to help me! They can't wait for me to fall in love."

Then I went on to explain that the Universe was no different than any of her best friends. The Universe wants Jessica to fall in love and wants nothing more than for her to be happy. I told her to chill out and revisit her Manifesting Equation with a more relaxed attitude. I suggested she connect with the Universe as if they were best friends who wanted to support one another's desires. She dug this idea, and it really helped her chill out. Don't block yourself from attracting by being impatient. Know that everything you want is on the way, and if you don't get what you want, it's because the Universe has a better plan.

CHAPTER TWELVE

Adding More ~ing
to Your Life

All fear is past and only love is here.
Can you imagine what it means to have no cares, no worries, no anxieties, but
merely to be perfectly calm and quiet all the time?
—A Course in Miracles

The key to happiness is the decision to be happy.
—A Return to Love *by Marianne Williamson*

When I was thirteen I performed a monologue from *The Diary of Anne Frank* in front of an audience of strangers. I don't remember much about the actual performance itself or the rehearsal leading up to it. What I do remember is the way I felt after reciting the words of Anne Frank's diary on stage. What I felt was an overwhelming sense of certainty that there was a more beautiful way to view the world than the way I currently perceived it. I felt as though my adolescent mini-dramas were ridiculous in comparison to this "other way" of living. However, the monologue resonated with me on a level I could not truly understand until many years later.

The Anne Frank monologue began with her happily looking up through a skylight at a beautiful sky. It was incredible that she could find joy, given her desperate situation of hiding from the Nazis. Trapped in an attic, somehow Anne Frank had found her way out. She tells her companion Peter that when she can't stand being cooped up for another moment, she *thinks* herself out of the situation, imagining herself walking in a park, a place "where the daffodils and the crocus and the violets grow down the slopes." Anne explained that the most wonderful thing about thinking your way out is that you can do it all the time. In the midst of terror, Anne Frank had found her ~*ing*.

She had discovered the most powerful tool a human could access—the power of her mind. By connecting to her ~*ing* she could choose love in an instant and become free of all worldly fear. Anne Frank had learned what the *Course* teaches: that "only love is real." She had a choice each day to choose the fear of the Holocaust or choose the love of her ~*ing*. Anne Frank chose love.

Through her dedication to love, she found faith. Her monologue concluded with how she thought the world was just "going through a phase." She spoke of her faith in the kindness of people and in the belief that all the terror would pass. She said, "I still believe, in spite of everything, that people are really good at heart." Having chosen love over fear she'd found hope in the loving voice of her *inner guide*.

Regardless of my age and my surroundings, I felt connected to Anne Frank's faith. I felt inspired by her vision. I felt her spirit touch me with a gentle reminder to release idle thoughts and choose the loving voice of my *inner guide*. At the age of fifteen, Anne Frank had an inner knowingness that choosing happiness was the best way to live. Even though she was caught up in the most horrific of circumstances, she chose to see the world through love rather than fear.

There have been many instances throughout my life in which Anne Frank's inspiration has intervened with my ego. For me, it was from early adolescence to the age of twenty-five that my ego's nightmare deepened. During that time in my life, I felt lost, disconnected, out of control, angry and fearful of everything and everyone. I was stuck in fears from the past and obsessed with fears of the future. I was living in the dark with a constant nagging feeling that there had to be a better way to live. A way of living I'd known before but had somehow lost touch with. I had a desire to get back to that better way.

It was right before I hit my personal rock bottom that I felt a strong pull to return to the words of Anne Frank. So one day I began rereading her diary. As I read the hope-filled passages of the young girl who chose to live in the light even during the darkest of times, I found inspiration in every word. One passage in particular struck me: "Everyone has inside of him a piece of good news. The good news is that you don't know how great you can be! How much you can love! What you can accomplish! And what your potential is!" Reading this, I felt as though she was speaking directly to me. In retrospect, I realize that she was. Indeed, at the time I had the strong desire and the openness to see life differently, and with that openness, I was guided to her words as a source of inspiration.

By choosing to see her world through the eyes of her *inner guide*, Anne Frank was able to find light and miracles while in hiding from the Nazis' terror. Anne Frank's dedication to her *inner guide* ignited my quest for happiness and inspired me to change my life. The loving energy behind her words reminded me that the love and happiness I was seeking on the outside was actually only available to me on the inside.

As a result of this divine intervention, I got on the right path and ultimately reconnected with my ~*ing*, and dedicated my life to it. Day by day I added up more ~*ing*. And day by day I got closer and closer to the "happy dream." (The *Course* teaches that the "happy dream" is when your mind has chosen to correct the fear and suffering of the ego and begin to see beyond its illusions.) I realized that each instant I am alive is a new opportunity to turn my will and my life over to my ~*ing* and allow myself to be guided.

Now, each day, I am willing to choose light over darkness. I'm grateful that I left my ego's attack of darkness and chose to see the light. Each day, I wake even more dedicated to seeing life through the light of my ~*ing*. I keep asking and I keep receiving. I will never turn my back on my *inner guide*. Like my dear friend Anne, I too am committed to the light.

Anne Frank continues to inspire me to this day. Tellingly, while I was wrapping up this book, I turned to my ~*ing* for guidance. I asked, "How can I send readers off in the final chapter? How can I encourage them in the last chapter to always choose the light?" I heard my *inner guide* say, "Remind them of Anne Frank." Tears welled up in my eyes as I was reconnected with her faith. Then and there I realized that there is really no better example to guide you toward the light.

And so, Anne Frank's faith in humanity and peace are what I want to leave you with in this chapter. Recognize her conscious decision to see the light in the midst of endless darkness. Her decision to choose the loving voice of her *inner guide* to carry her out of the darkness that had befallen the world. The evidence of her choice can be found in passages throughout her beautiful diary, passages such as, "I don't think of all the misery, but of the beauty that still remains . . ." Anne Frank's faithful commitment to happiness is what led her to live in the "happy dream" rather than the darkness that became her reality. What inspires me most is how, in the midst of the horrifying darkness, she *chose* to see the light.

That's what I ask of you today. Choose to see the light over the ego's darkness. Regardless of your life's circumstances, there is always a loving view open to you. You can make the decision to *choose* to see the light over the darkness at any moment. Start slowly if you have to. Wake up tomorrow morning and decide to be happy for a full twenty-four hours. For a full day, *choose* to see every situation with a loving perspective, regardless of how difficult it may seem at first glance. Each time someone does something to upset you, *choose* to forgive them. When a fearful thought arises, turn it over to your ~*ing* to be transformed back to love. Release future outcomes and focus on the love in the present moment. Then wake up the next day and do it all over again. Day by day, add up your ~*ing*.

As a result of adding up your ~*ing*, you'll know you're being guided and that the Universe has your back. You'll expect miracles to occur each time you change your mind. Even better, you will inspire those around you because you'll be vibrating at such a positive frequency. Great stuff will flow to you effortlessly, and you will be happy.

That sounds good, right? Well, I'll let you in on some exciting news; *you*, my friend, already know how to access your ~*ing*, and you know what to do on a moment-by-moment basis to experience a state of happy flow. Each instant that you've chosen ~*ing* over ego has led you closer to the light and into a happier state of mind. With your commitment to each ~*ing* Equation, you've smothered the darkness of your ego with the light of your *inner guide*. You have joined me on a journey of bringing your darkness to the light. But don't stop now! I ask that after you close this book and set it aside, you continue your ~*ing* work. Give yourself permission to live with the light of your *inner guide* all the time!

The goal of this chapter is to line you up to choose ~*ing* over ego in every instant. As a result, you will be led to the "happy dream." This is the state of mind I described above in Anne Frank's story. In the "happy dream," you live in happiness and choose to experience life through the eyes of love, regardless of how difficult your life's circumstances may be. When you choose this way of life, you are no longer willing to play small. You are ready to own your power, own your happiness and live in the light.

WORK*ing* MIRACLES

The *Course* writes, "The darkness in you has been brought to the light." By choosing the happiness of the light, you've chosen to be a miracle worker. By shifting your perception on a moment-by-moment basis, you've created miracles in your own life and in the lives of others. Whether you know it or not, your shift in energy has been changing the world around you. Your friends might have noticed these changes in you and as a result decided to check out this ~*ing* thing themselves. Or you may have forgiven someone and as a result your relationship with them is much more loving. All of these miracles have positively affected you, the people around you, and the world. Keep adding up the miracles. By doing so, you *will* join me in the "happy dream."

You might be thinking, "That sounds super nice, but it's easy for her to say. She lives for this *happy* stuff." That's just your ego talking. Your ego will attempt to stop you from being a miracle worker and try to stand in the way of your living a happy life. The ego will say things like, "Who are you to be happy? You can't live this way! You can't just live in a happy state of mind."

Choose not to listen. By now you know to expect this kind of ego backlash any time you turn toward the light. Now that you're aware of the ego's bag of tricks, you have two options: choose the light of your ~*ing* or the darkness of your ego. It's one thing to choose your ~*ing* when life is tough and you've hit bottom, but it's entirely another to choose it all the time. If you're considering the light, ask yourself the following questions: *Are you willing to change your life and choose your ~ing over your ego at every instant? Are you willing to forgive everything and everyone around you whenever necessary? Are you willing to be happy?* If you've answered "yes," then you are ready to add even more ~*ing* to your life.

Choosing THE "Happy Dream"

You *can* add up enough ~*ing* to live in the "happy dream." Simply be willing to make the choice to do so. Make a choice to release the ego and stop playing small. Humbly laugh at the ego's silly stories. And ask for help to release your fearful mind. By communicating with your ~*ing*, you can release your ego in an instant. This is what the *Course* calls the "holy instant." Each ~*ing* Equation guides you toward the "holy instant." These instants are simple. They are the moments in time when you're willing to offer your ego to your ~*ing* for transformation. As a result, you feel an immediate sense of relief and an alignment with your true loving essence. Turn every issue in your life over to your ~*ing*. This dedication to ~*ing* thinking doesn't mean you'll never experience a fearful thought. Instead you just experience fear differently by choosing love instead.

Adding More ~*ing*

The *Course* teaches that "An untrained mind can accomplish nothing." Now that you have the ~*ing* tools in your back pocket, don't deny them. Tap into your ~*ing* to help you retrain your mind. The more you retrain your mind, the closer you get to the "happy dream." The first step is to be will*ing*. Your will*ingness* will guide the process and set you up to play big. Next you'll use the rethink*ing* step to learn how to choose the "holy instant." By choosing the "holy instant," you let your ~*ing* to do its thing. Then, you'll mix mov*ing* with your new affirmation: "I am will*ing* to turn all of my fears over to the care of my *inner guide*." You can apply this affirmation to any form of movement. Just ~*ing* with it. Then you'll be led into a meditation where you'll further align your thoughts with your *inner guide*. In your meditation you can bring any issue to your ~*ing* for healing. All that's required of you is faith and stillness. Allow your ~*ing* to guide you through this transformational meditation. Finally you'll ~*ing write* about your miracles. You'll document the work you've done and the miraculous shifts you've created. Keep this ~*ing write* in a folder so that you can refer to it for inspiration at any time.

THE ADD*ing* MORE ~*ing* EQUATION

STEP ONE: Willing

Be willing to see the world through Anne's lenses, with her words like, "I've found that there is always some beauty left—in nature, sunshine, freedom, in yourself; these can help you. Look at these things, then find yourself again, and God, and then you regain your balance." Before you begin using the tools in the Add*ing* More ~*ing* Equation, I encourage you to set your intention to the Universe. Simply say out loud, *"I am willing to turn all of my fears over to the care of my inner guide."* By setting this intention from the get-go, you are immediately lining yourself up for a radical ~*ing* ride. Hold tight and expect miracles.

STEP TWO: Rethink*ing*: Choosing a "Holy Instant"

Forgiving
Begin the rethink*ing* step by forgiving the ego's thoughts. In this step your ~*ing* will listen and guide you to be nonjudgmental, patient and gentle with your ego. By perceiving your ego as a sick dog off the leash, you'll choose to stay calm and be able to laugh at the ego's mischief. The key to experiencing a "holy instant" is to be aware of the ego's power.

Pick Up the Phone and Call Your Inner Guide
Stay alert to the moment your ego starts in with fear of the past and future. Rather than succumb to fear, you can shift gears and recognize the ego's attack. When you feel your ~*ing* is threatened by anything, stop instantly, pick up your cell phone and make a phone call to your *inner guide*. Literally pick up the phone. This is a great action for when you are in the office, on the street or anywhere that's public. The cell phone allows you to speak out loud without looking like a freak. Pick up your phone, pretend to dial, and ask your *inner guide* to exchange this fear for a more peaceful thought. Say out loud, *"I choose to forgive and see this situation with love. Inner guide, please transform my thoughts and vision."*

Trusting
Having faith in your *inner guide* is key to creating the "holy instant." If you find your ego starts to trip you up along the way, turn to the *Course's* quote for help. Simply say out loud, *"Trust would settle every problem now."* Allow this message from the *Course* to act as a gentle reminder to have full faith in your ~*ing*, knowing that it will always be your guide.

STEP THREE: Rethinking + Moving

Go dancing, climbing, rebounding, unicycling, hiking, swimming, walking, running, trapeze flying, rollerblading, anything, just get moving! And don't forget to bring your ~ing affirmations with you from now on. Bring your affirmation *I am willing to turn all of my fears over to the care of my inner guide*, and embark on a journey toward the "happy dream." Welcome miracles with each adventure and have fun!

STEP FOUR: Receiving (Meditating/~ing write)

Meditating

The crucial step in creating the "holy instant" is to bring your ego to your *inner guide* for healing through meditation. As soon as you choose to see your issue through the eyes of your ~ing, sit in a meditation and allow your *inner guide* to get to work. That "holy instant" is created in the midst of a meditation where you surrender your ego to your ~ing and ask for help. Just relax and let your thoughts be transformed. If you need to focus on something, simply recite your mantra, *I am willing to turn all of my fears over to the care of my inner guide*. Continue to repeat this mantra until you feel a shift.

~ing write

Following your meditation ~ing write about the experience. Take note of how your thoughts shifted and how your mind softened. Honor all shifts, big or small. Remember what the *Course* teaches us: "There is no order of difficulty in miracles." Each shift is a miracle; honor them all.

Finally, ~ing write for fifteen minutes, reflecting on all of the miracles you've added up throughout your ~ing journey thus far.

Be proud of the miraculous changes you've made. Love yourself for fearlessly crossing over the bridge from your old life into the "happy dream."

Now, my dear friend, I must send you on your way. I thank you for beginning this journey with me. I encourage you to continue ~*inging* forever. Know that at any moment you can ask for a miracle and choose to see your world through loving lenses. I honor you for your dedication to your *inner guide*. I wrap you with love and send you off with a final message from the *Course:* "Who would attempt to fly with the tiny wings of a sparrow when the mighty power of an eagle has been given him?"

Share light. Expect miracles. Honor the voice of your *inner guide*.

—The Beginn*ing*